HighTide and Nottingham Playhouse Theatre Company present

LIT

by Sophie Ellerby

LIT was first performed as a co-production between HighTide and
Nottingham Playhouse at HighTide Festival, Aldeburgh in September 2019

LIT
by Sophie Ellerby

BEX	Eve Austin
DILLON	Josh Barrow
RUTH	Tiger Cohen-Towell
SYLVIA	Maxine Finch
LEE	Kieran Hardcastle
MARK	Jim Pope

Director	Stef O'Driscoll
Designer	Minglu Wang
Lighting Designer	Peter Small
Sound Designer	Dominic Kennedy
Movement Director	Hayley Chilvers
Fight Director	Jonathan Holby
Casting Director	Vicky Richardson CDG
Production Manager	Jill Robertshaw
Stage Management	Amber Jane Taylor

CAST

EVE AUSTIN | BEX

Eve recently wrapped filming on *Our Ladies* for Sony directed by Michael Caton-Jones and produced by Sigma Films. Other recent credits include a leading role in *The ABC Murders* alongside John Malkovich for the BBC & Amazon Prime and *The Athena* for Sky. Eve trained at the prestigious Nottingham Television Workshop.

JOSH BARROW | DILLON

Originally from Newcastle, Josh made the move to London in 2017. He is an active member of the National Youth Theatre after completing the Epic Stages course in 2015. Since beginning his professional career, he has written and produced his own play with his company Gutter Street and gained the title of TriForce's Monologue Slam National Champion after competing with a self-penned piece.

Theatre includes: *Silk Road – How to Buy Drugs Online* (Trafalgar Studios); *The Outsider* (The Print Room); *If Not Now, When?* (National Theatre). Television includes: *Temple*; *Vera*. Film includes: *The Trap*; *My Brother Is A Mermaid*.

TIGER COHEN-TOWELL | RUTH

Tiger trained at the Television Workshop in Nottingham, where she appeared in productions including *Primadonna* and Sophie Ellerby's *Crabs*.

Short film includes *Wash Club*, *Ariella* and *Crush*, and spots for Confetti, Childline and NSPCC.

Tiger is currently part of a two-piece band called Megatrain; writing, recording and performing primarily in Nottingham and London, with play on BBC6Music.

She has been involved with the development of *LIT* from its beginnings, and appeared in the HighTide production in 2017.

MAXINE FINCH I SYLVIA

Maxine Finch trained at Dartington College of Arts.

Television includes: *Coronation Street; Hollyoaks; Vera; Moving On; DCI Banks; Emmerdale; Eternal Law; Waterloo Road; Blue Murder; The Good Samaritan; Strictly Confidential; New Street Law; Doctors; Guardian; Holby City; Spine Chillers; Burn It; Crossroads* and *Dangerfield.*

Film includes: *Provoked; A Change in the Weather; The Silver Mask.*

Theatre includes: *State Red* (Hampstead Theatre); *The Crucible* (Welsh National Theatre); *Precious* (Theatre Centre); *Unsent Letters & In Balance* (Hearth Theatre); *Skybus* (Derby Live); *Getting it Straight* (The Works); *Inside Out Of Mind* (Meeting Ground); and *All Different, All Equal* (Women in Theatre).

KIERAN HARDCASTLE I LEE

A graduate of the award-winning Nottingham Television Workshop, Kieran's credits include playing antagonist Saul in E4's acclaimed *My Mad Fat Diary;* Kes in BAFTA award-winning film *This is England* and Martin Dowling in season 6 of *Waterloo Road.* As well as featuring in the successful short films *Wish 143;* Beverley and Jimmy McGovern's hit series *Accused;* Kieran recently appeared in *Bohemian Rhapsody* having dialogue with Academy award winner Rami Malek.

As a writer, Kieran has had work optioned by Hat Trick Productions and play at the London Short Film Festival (opening film).

JIM POPE I MARK

Jim Pope is the Artistic Director of Playing ON theatre company, bringing together mental health staff and service users to create theatre. He directed and acted in *Hearing Things* by Philip Osment at Omnibus Theatre, Clapham.

Other theatre includes Mr Gryce, Mr Farthing and Mr Sugden in *Kes* at CAST. With Mike Alfreds' Method and Madness ensemble he performed as Andrew in *Buried Alive* by Philip Osment, Firs in *The Cherry Orchard* by Chekhov, Vogel in *The Black Dahlia* by James Elroy and The Narrator in *Demons and Dybbuks* by Isaac Bashevis Singer.

TV includes *The Bill, Doctors, Casualty* and *Impact* (directed by John Strickland).

CREATIVES

SOPHIE ELLERBY | WRITER

Sophie is a Midlands playwright. She joined the Nottingham Television Workshop as a teenager and began her career as an actor. When she was awarded a place on HighTide's First Commission scheme in 2016 she wrote her debut play *LIT*. Other work includes *THREE*, performed at the Arcola theatre in 2017 and both *Function* and *crabs* for the National Youth Theatre. She is currently under commission to the National Youth Theatre and Fifth Word Theatre and is this year's Writer in Residence at Pentabus Theatre. Sophie is dedicated to working on projects that challenge social norms and ignite community imagination. Her plays tackle provocative societal questions in an accessible and human way.

STEF O'DRISCOLL | DIRECTOR

Stef is the Artistic Director of nabokov and previously the Associate Director at Paines Plough and at the Lyric Hammersmith.

For Paines Plough: *Daughterhood* by Charley Miles; *On The Other Hand, We're Happy* by Daf James; *Dexter and Winter's Detective Agency* by Nathan Bryon; *Sticks and Stones* by Vinay Patel; *Island Town* by Simon Longman; *With A Little Bit Of Luck* by Sabrina Mahfouz; *Hopelessly Devoted* by Kate Tempest; *Blister* by Laura Lomas; and as Assistant Director: *Wasted* by Kate Tempest.

For nabokov: *Last Night* by Benin City (Roundhouse/Latitude); *Box Clever* by Monsay Whitney (Marlowe Theatre/Roundabout/Bunker); *Storytelling Army* (Brighton Festival) and *Slug* by Sabrina Mahfouz (Latitude).

For the Lyric, as Co Director: *A Midsummer Night's Dream*; as Associate Director: *Mogadishu* (Manchester Royal Exchange); as Assistant Director: *Blasted* – winner Olivier Award for Outstanding Achievement in an Affiliate Theatre 2011.

Other Director credits: *Yard Gal* by Rebecca Prichard – winner Fringe Report Awards for Best Fringe Production 2009 (Oval House); *A Tale From The Bedsit* by Paul Cree (Roundhouse/Bestival); *Finding Home* by Cecilia Knapp (Roundhouse); *A Guide To Second Date Sex* and *When Women Wee* (Underbelly/Soho) and as Assistant Director: *Henry IV* (Donmar/St Anne's Warehouse).

MINGLU WANG | DESIGNER

Minglu Wang is a scenographer who likes to explore materials, body, space and performance. She graduated from Royal Central School of Speech and Drama with Distinction and has a background of BA theatre, film and Television art designing. She works nationally and internationally and her work has featured in festivals including the Prague Quadrennial of Performance Design and Space 2011 and London Art Biennale 2015. She was a Linbury Prize finalist, winner of Taking the Stage 2015 supported by British Council Ukraine, and was a selected designer at World Stage Design 2017, Taipei. She is also a visiting professional at the Central School of Speech and Drama.

PETER SMALL | LIGHTING DESIGNER

Peter is an Offie and Theatre & Technology Award nominated lighting designer working across theatre, dance and opera.

Recent credits include *Square Go* (Roundabout and New York); *Angry Alan* (Soho Theatre and Aspen Fringe); *Baby Reindeer, Do Our Best* (Francesca Moody Productions Edinburgh Fringe); *Radio* (Arcola); *Ad Libido* (VAULT Festival, Edinburgh Fringe and Soho Theatre); *YOU STUPID DARKNESS!* (Theatre Royal Plymouth); Paines Plough Roundabout Tour productions 2017–19, including the Offie Nominated *Black Mountain*; *A Girl In School Uniform (walks into a bar)* (Offie and Theatre & Technology Award Nominated – New Diorama) and *All or Nothing* (West End and tour).

Upcoming shows include *Spiderfly* for Theatre 503 and transferring *Baby Reindeer* to Bush Theatre, among others.

DOMINIC KENNEDY | SOUND DESIGNER

Dominic Kennedy is a sound designer and music producer for performance and live events; he has a keen interest in developing new work and implementing sound and music at an early stage in a creative process. Dominic is a graduate from Royal Central School of Speech and Drama, where he developed specialist skills in collaborative and devised theatre making, music composition and installation practices. His work often fuses found sound, field recordings, music composition and synthesis.

Recent design credits include: Roundabout Season 2019 (Paines Plough); *YOU STUPID DARKNESS!* (Paines Plough/Theatre Royal Plymouth); *Pop Music* (Paines Plough/Birmingham REP/Latitude); *Skate Hard Turn Left* (Battersea Arts Centre); Roundabout Season 2019 (Paines Plough/Theatr Clwyd); *Angry Alan* (Soho); *The Assassination of Katie Hopkins* (Theatr Clwyd); *With A Little Bit Of Luck* (Paines Plough/BBC Radio 1Xtra); *Ramona Tells Jim* (Bush Theatre); *And The Rest of Me Floats* (Outbox Theatre); *I Am A Tree* (Jamie Wood); *Box Clever* (nabokov).

HAYLEY CHILVERS | MOVEMENT DIRECTOR

Hayley has extensive experience working as a dancer for physical theatre, dance and opera companies. Choreographers Hayley has worked with include, Rosie Whitney-Fish, Taira Foo, Natasha Kamjani, Katie Pearson and Kerry Fletcher.

She has also worked with director Mark Murphy on the Cricket World Cup Opening Ceremony as a dancer and then as a choreography consultant for the ball boys and girls on his latest production of *Rematch*, an immersive recreation of the Wimbledon tennis final between Borg and McEnroe produced by Wimbledon.

Hayley works as dancer and rehearsal director for The Natashas Project, an international physical theatre charity founded in 2013. Its aim is to use dance to inform and equip the public about Human Trafficking and Modern Day Slavery and support survivors through creative means by providing restorative workshops at safe houses across London.

Hayley worked with Anna Morrissey during the creation of *On Progress* for Historic Royal Palaces at Hampton Court which she also later helped to revive as Anna's rehearsal director. She then went on to work with Anna for an initial research and development phase, helping to create movement for Emilia which was first performed at the Globe and then went on to the West End at the Vaudeville Theatre.

Hayley most recently worked with Stef O'Driscoll as associate movement director for Paines Plough on their Roundabout productions which are currently touring the UK, she is delighted to be working with Stef again on *LIT*.

JONATHAN HOLBY I FIGHT DIRECTOR
Jonathan Holby is a London-based Fight Director.

Recent work includes: *Coram Boy, The Memory of Water* and *The Madness Of George III* (Nottingham Playhouse); *Legend Trippers* (The Other Palace – NYMT); *Romeo and Juliet* (Shakespeare's Rose Theatre – Blenheim); *Hamlet, Twelfth Night* and *The Tempest* (Shakespeare's Rose Theatre – York); *Waitress* (Adelphi Theatre); *Fight Night* (The Vaults); *Summer and Smoke* (Duke of York Theatre); *West Side Story* (Cambridge Theatre Company); *Midnight* (Union Theatre/ Korea); *Macbeth* and *A Midsummer Night's Dream* (Shakespeare's Rose Theatre); *The King and I* (London Palladium); *Machinal* (Almeida Theatre).

Film includes: *Lily, Damned, School Swordman, My Mother, Work, Crossed* and *Hal*.

VICKY RICHARDSON CDG I CASTING DIRECTOR
Vicky is currently Associate Casting Director at the Royal Exchange Theatre, Manchester and was previously Casting Associate at Donmar Warehouse.

Credits as Casting Director include: *Town Mouse and Country Mouse* (Nottingham Playhouse); *Of Kith and Kin* (Crucible Theatre, Sheffield/Bush Theatre); *Desire Under the Elms* (Crucible Theatre, Sheffield); *Macbeth; Romeo and Juliet; I Want My Hat Back* (National Theatre); *Breaking the Code* (Royal Exchange Theatre, Manchester); *Run the Beast Down* (Finborough Theatre); *Henry IV* (Donmar Warehouse/St Ann's Warehouse); *Constellations* (Singapore Repertory Theatre); *House/Amongst the Reeds* (Clean Break); *Archipelago* (Lighthouse, Poole); *Dinner with Friends* (Park Theatre); *Debris* (Southwark Playhouse).

Credits as Co-Casting Director include: *Our Town; Persuasion; Twelfth Night* (Royal Exchange Theatre, Manchester); *Parliament Square* (Royal Exchange Theatre, Manchester/Bush Theatre); *The Resistible Rise of Arturo Ui; Versailles* (Donmar Warehouse); *Shakespeare Trilogy* (Donmar Warehouse/St Ann's Warehouse); *Dedication* (Nuffield Southampton Theatres).

Credits as Casting Consultant include: *Misalliance; Low Level Panic; Each His Own Wilderness; Buckets* (Orange Tree Theatre); *Blue Heart* (Tobacco Factory, Bristol/Orange Tree Theatre).

Special thanks to **Podders Nottingham Ltd.**

HIGH TIDE

NEW THEATRE FOR
ADVENTUROUS PEOPLE

HighTide is a theatre company and charity based in East Anglia that has an unparalleled twelve-year history of successfully launching the careers of emerging British playwrights.

Our alumni speak for themselves: Luke Barnes, Adam Brace, Tallulah Brown, E V Crowe, Elinor Cook, Rob Drummond, Thomas Eccleshare, Theresa Ikoko, Branden Jacobs-Jenkins, Eve Leigh, Anders Lustgarten, Joel Horwood, Ella Hickson, Harry Melling, Nessah Muthy, Vinay Patel, Nick Payne, Phil Porter, Beth Steel, Al Smith, Sam Steiner, Molly Taylor, Jack Thorne and Frances Ya-Chu Cowhig.

We have staged productions with the highest quality theatres across the UK, from the Traverse in Edinburgh, to the Royal Exchange in Manchester, Theatre Royal Bath and the National Theatre in London. We discover new talent, provide creative development opportunities for playwrights and other creatives, and stage high quality theatre productions both in our region and nationally through our festivals and touring.

We enable new and underrepresented playwrights to express their visions of contemporary politics and society, demonstrate their creative potential and therein showcase the future of theatre.

LANSONS
Advice Ideas Results

HIGH TIDE

2019
TWELVE YEARS OF SHAPING THE MAINSTREAM

Our twelfth season under Artistic Director Steven Atkinson, began in February 2019 with Eve Leigh's **The Trick**, directed by Roy Alexander Weise in a HighTide and Loose Tongue co-production. **The Trick** premiered at the Bush Theatre before embarking on an national tour.

In April, **Mouthpiece** by Kieran Hurley, presented by Traverse Theatre in association with HighTide transfered to Soho Theatre after a successful run at Traverse Theatre in December 2018. It will return to Edinburgh in August as part of the Traverse's Edinburgh Festival Fringe 2019 season.

Rust by Kenny Emson, directed by Eleanor Rhode, was presented in a HighTide and Bush Theatre co-production in June 2019 at the Bush Theatre. **Rust** transferred to the Edinburgh Festival Fringe before running at HighTide Festival in September 2019.

HighTide, in partnership with Assembly Roxy, launched **Disruption: The Future of New Theatre** as part of the Edinburgh Festival Fringe 2019. **Disruption** presented a curated programme of provocative and contemporary new theatre. Alongside **Rust**, HighTide has co-produce a further four productions: **Pops** by Charlotte Josephine, **Collapsible** by Margaret Perry, **Since U Been Gone** by Teddy Lamb & **Pink Lemonade** by Mika Johnson.

Former HighTide First Commissions Writer Sophie Ellerby premieres **LIT** in September 2019, directed by Stef O'Driscoll in a HighTide and Nottingham Playhouse co-production. **LIT** debuts at the HighTide Festival before transferring to Omnibus Clapham and Nottingham Playhouse.

Finally, HighTide are partnering with **BBC Radio 3** and **BBC Arts** on two new radio plays by HighTide alumni writers Tallulah Brown and Vinay Patel. These plays will be presented at HighTide Festival in 2019 with a live recording to be broadcast later this year.

HIGH TIDE

HIGHTIDE THEATRE

24a St John Street, London, EC1M 4AY
0207 566 9765 - hello@hightide.org.uk - hightide.org.uk

HighTide Company

Artistic Director Steven Atkinson
Artistic Director Designate Suba Das
Executive Producer Francesca Clark
Executive Producer (Maternity Cover) Rowan Rutter
Producer Robyn Keynes
Assistant Producer Holly White
Festival Producer, Aldeburgh Elizabeth Downie
Marketing and Communications Officer Kathleen Smith

Associate Writers:
Taj Atwal, William Drew, Sonia Jalaly, James McDermott, Yolanda Mercy

Board
Steven Atkinson; Tim Clark (Chair); Nancy Durrant; Sue Emmas; Liz Fosbury; Jon Gilchrist; Diana Hiddleston; Priscilla John; Clare Parsons; Vinay Patel; John Rodgers; Leah Schmidt; Graham White (Deputy Chair)

Festival Board, Aldeburgh
Tallulah Brown; Andrew Clarke; Tim Clark (HighTide chair); Heather Newill; Ruth Proctor; Jenni Wake-Walker; Caroline Wiseman

Patrons
Stephen Daldry CBE; Sir Richard Eyre CBE; Sally Greene OBE; Sir David Hare; Sir Nicholas Hytner; Sam Mendes CBE; Juliet Stevenson CBE.

H|GH T|DE

BE A FRIEND OF THE FESTIVAL

"There are very talented young playwrights in the UK and if they are lucky they will find their way to HighTide Theatre. I hope you will join me in supporting this remarkable and modest organisation. With your help HighTide can play an even more major role in the promoting of new writing in the UK."
Lady Susie Sainsbury, Backstage Trust

Our Friends are an important part of HighTide. Our benefits include:
- An invite to the Festival programme launch party in Aldeburgh
- An invite to the Artists and Friends Brunch during the Festival
- Dedicated ticket booking service and access to house seats for sold out events

From as little as £10 a month, your contribution will support the Festival in providing:
- Performance tickets to local school children
- Workshops on performance and writing
- The Summer Connect club in Aldeburgh for the next generation of playwrights

All of which we can provide at no cost to local young people, thanks to the generosity of our Friends.

Be a Friend for as little as £10 per month, or become a Best Friend for as little as £25 per month.

To make a one-off contribution, please call our offices on 01728 687110 quoting `Friends of the Festival', or email **rowan@hightide.org.uk**.

We are thankful to all of our supporters, without whom our work simply would not take place.

HighTide Theatre is a National Portfolio Organisation of the Arts Council England

Nottingham Playhouse

Nottingham Playhouse is dedicated to making bold and thrilling world-class theatre in the heart of Nottingham and was named Regional Theatre of the Year in The Stage Awards 2019.

Autumn 2019 productions include *An Enemy of the People* starring Alex Kingston, Stephen Sondheim's Tony Award-winning musical satire *Assassins* and *LIT* by Nottingham playwright Sophie Ellerby.

Nottingham Playhouse's 2018 production of *The Madness of George III* was one of the first to be broadcast internationally by National Theatre Live from a theatre outside of London and won the WhatsOnStage Awards for Best Play Revival and Best Supporting Actor in a Play (for Adrian Scarborough's performance as Dr Willis). Both *Shebeen* (commissioned by Nottingham Playhouse) and *Lava* from spring 2018 were world premieres, with *Shebeen* also winning the Alfred Fagon Award.

Nottingham Playhouse's productions tour nationally and internationally. Its revival of *Wonderland* toured to Newcastle in spring 2019 and its production of *One Night in Miami...* visited Bristol Old Vic and HOME Manchester in summer 2019.

Nottingham Playhouse believes theatre should be accessible to all, and runs wide-reaching participation schemes, youth theatres and its Amplify programme, which seeks to inspire and supprt theatre-makers from the East Midlands.

Chief Executive **Stephanie Sirr**
Artistic Director **Adam Penford**

'Adam Penford [is] running and thoroughly reinvigorating
Nottingham Playhouse' *The Telegraph*

'The last 12 months has seen Nottingham Playhouse re-energised.
Under the leadership of Chief Executive Stephanie Sirr and new Artistic Director
Adam Penford, the theatre... has been revitalised creatively.'
The Stage citation for Regional Theatre of the Year 2019 Award

Nottingham Playhouse Theatre Company

Directors
Stephanie Sirr
Adam Penford

Administration
Valerie Evans
Liz Johnson
Laura Guthrie
Andrew Bullett
Frances Pearson

Artist Development
Craig Gilbert
Lewis Doherty
Major Labia
Ben Norris

Associate Artists
James Graham
Sarah 'Rain' Kolawole
Amanda Whittington
Matthew Xia

Box Office
Richard Surgay
Jonathan Davies
Matt Smith
Jeremy Walker
Edward Jones
Gary Miller

Cleaning & Maintenance
Michael Turton
Cindy Hutchinson
William Goodman
Michael Parnham
Patricia Walsh
Paul White

Construction
Julian Smith
Philip Gunn
Suelin Webster

Digital Production
Fraser Youngson

Finance
Rachel Amery
Jonathan Child
Sara Oakden
Abbie Lloyd

Front of House
Tracy James
Stewart Smith
Isla Kay
Ollie Smith
Rob Throup
Christine Baxter

Lisa Booth-Blake
Pamela Bullett
Sophie Curtis
Olwen Davies
Clare Devine
Stacey Foster
Kristy Guest
Bill Henshaw
Chris Howitt
Dale Hurren
Laura Hutchinson
Clare Johnson
Lydia Jones
Imogen Lea
Georgie Levers
Richard Marson
Emily Owen
Paul Preston
Dave Richardson
Matthew Smith
Wesley Smith
Sally Smithson
Andrew Tinley

Fundraising & Development
Olivia Wood

Lighting, Sound & Video
Karl Bock
Will Cottrell
Will Welch
Bethany Shaw
Richard Warriner

Marketing & Communications
Joanna Sigsworth
Chloe McMackin
Hollie Anderson
Derek Graham
Rebecca Hogarth
Charli Blighton
Alessandra Doogan
David Burns PR

Paintshop
Claire Thompson
Emily Hackett

Participation
Martin Berry
Elaine Williamson
Beth Morris
Manya Benenson
Dawn Richmond-Gordon

Production
Andy Bartlett
Jill Robertshaw

Props
Nathan Rose
Alex Hatton

Stage Door
Louise Carney
Olwen Davies
Kristy Guest
Geoff Linney
Paul Preston
Dave Richardson
Ollie Smith
Susan Yeoman

Stage Management
Jane Eliot-Webb
Vickki Maiden
Kathryn Bainbridge-Wilson

Technical
Jamie Smith
Tony Topping
Kushal Patel

Wardrobe
Helen Tye
Linda Burrows
Emma Greenhalgh
Michelle Bland
Heather Flinders

Access Services
Stefanie Bell
Rebekah Cupit
Alison Green
Jane Edwards
Sally Goulding
Derek Graham
Tullia Randall
Katie Yapp

Neville Studio Volunteers
Ilija Barosevcic
Karl Bloch
Richard Brown
Louise Carney
Claire Long
Susan MacCormick
Charlie Middlemiss
Abby Riddell
Katy Taylor
Ellie Torrance
Olivia Trivett

LIT

Sophie Ellerby

For Mum, always. Thank you for giving me faith.

*And for the mums inside, currently serving time.
We must not forget you.*

Author's Note

LIT is set in the East Midlands, Nottinghamshire. The story takes place in various locations during Bex's teenage years; semi-detached houses, comprehensive school, village halls, a few fields, a shitload of hormones and a lot of boredom to fill.

This piece explores the grey areas surrounding love and sex. It's important that the characters are neither portrayed as 'victims' or as 'perpetrators'. I have purposefully left a few unknowns in the text, however there are some important facts you need to consider when performing this play:

Bex just wants to be loved.

Lee isn't sexually attracted to Ruth.

Ruth doesn't remember what happened.

Dillon falls in love with Bex.

Bex tries to kiss Mark. Mark rejects Bex. At some point during that moment though, he did indeed 'think about it'.

Dillon and Lee are scarred for life.

The baby is Lee's.

Bex is convicted for arson with intent to endanger life, she pleads guilty. She is held on remand whilst awaiting sentencing. Taking into account the aggravating and mitigating factors – predominantly her age, the guilty plea and the impact of the rape (supported by a statement from Dillon) – her sentence is reduced from six years to four. With good behaviour Bex could serve fifty per cent of her sentence and be out in two years. At that point, she would be eighteen years old.

When producing this play, the safety of the actor playing Bex is paramount. Please be aware you have a duty of care for the actors, the creative team, and the audience.

S.E.

Characters

BEX, *fourteen to sixteen, bold, full of energy, vibrant, fearless, gobby, captivating, cheeky and restless. She may seem insensitive and brash but it all masks a very sensitive interior.*

RUTH, *fourteen to fifteen, guarded, intelligent, reserved, astute, sheltered, self-assured, measured, contemplative, sensitive and thoughtful. She becomes enamoured by Bex.*

SYLVIA, *forties, Bex's new foster mum. Scatty, well-meaning, airy, passionate, loving, a worrier, intense, warm, lonely, caring and insecure. She has a huge heart; sees Bex as her own.*

DILLON, *fifteen to sixteen, at school with Bex and Ruth, in the year above. Attempting a hard exterior but a complete softie really. Desperate to be accepted. The 'bad boy' at school, duty-bound to his family.*

LEE, *late twenties, Dillon's older brother. Cheeky geezer, filthy mouth, funny, intimidating. He could charm his way out of a bin bag. Makes himself known to everyone but really he's lonely as fuck.*

MARK, *forties, Ruth's dad. Reliable, trustworthy, charming, attractive, well-meaning but awkward. His daughter is his world.*

Note on Text

A dash (–) indicates either being interrupted or someone stopping their own thought (a full stop can also indicate this).

An ellipsis (...) indicates a trailing-off or searching for words.

A forward slash (/) indicates the point at which the next character starts speaking.

A new line communicates a new thought.

Words encased in square brackets [...] are not spoken.

The play should be performed without an interval.

This text went to press before the end of rehearsals and so may differ slightly from the play as performed.

BEX SAYS GOODBYE

BEX *stands next to a newborn baby in a plastic neonatal cot in hospital.*

BEX. This is it then.

If I don't cry, it don't mean I don't love you alright? It's just. Hard. Innit.

BEX *looks at her baby.*

Look when I get out, I reckon we should move to the countryside. Cos we could get chickens. Could ride ponies. All them sorta things what people do in the countryside, like gardening and stuff. In a little cottage or summit. Like three bears' cottage. With a straw roof. No, I know, it's mad innit? People seriously still live in them kinda houses though Amy, it's true. I saw it on *Location, Location, Location.*

Cos then you can go primary school near a farm and we can feed the ducks and stuff. Honestly, this episode was just like – oh my god, I want that. Kirsty and Phil were like totally biggin up this area, I think it were called Gloucestershire or summit. Proper countryside. With sheeps and cows and all that. Like proper.

But that's it innit. Nature and shit. That's what we need. We'll be dead free. And we won't have to be scared. Of anything.

Silence.

Dunno what I'm meant to say to ya. Not like you're gonna remember it so...

Just know that I'm gonna make it so much better for you. That's a promise. Cos it ain't been no fairytale for me Amy. Life.

Them stories that they tell ya, that they're gonna tell ya, when you start going school n that, when you start reading. They're a loada shite.

Cos they make out like princesses are so fucking perfect but. They're always waiting for some bloke to come and rescue them, like seriously, what is that about?

No one can save you in life 'part from yourself Amy, you hear that?

I could write better fairytales than that crap.

Beat.

Once upon a time there was this princess right. She were dead pretty. Obvs. Everyone knew who she was. She were basically famous.

And her name. Her name was…

BEX ISN'T HUNGRY

Mid-July. The last week of Year 9 before the summer holidays.

*A kitchen. Radio 4 is playing, it beeps signalling it's 8 a.m.,
followed swiftly by a news report. The table is laid for
breakfast; Coco Pops, a bowl, spoon and some milk in
a porcelain jug. BEX is sat dressed in a pink fluffy dressing
gown. SYLVIA enters in a hurry, doing three things at once.*

SYLVIA. Bex! Quickly. We're late.

> BEX *picks up the milk jug, sniffs it.* SYLVIA *takes a brown
> envelope out her bag, places in front of* BEX.

Money for the trip. Don't go spending it on sweets, or
cigarettes, or whatever.

BEX. I don't smoke.

> SYLVIA *gives her a look like 'you don't fool me'.*

SYLVIA. You're not even dressed yet! And I don't need another
phone call home. Remember what Miss Riley said about
uniform rules. To the knee.

> BEX *rolls her eyes.*

Maybe I'll go back to John Lewis and buy the other skirt.
The one with the pleats. One you can't roll up.

BEX. I'm not wearing that.

> SYLVIA*'s mobile starts to ring. She looks anxious and turns
> the radio off.*

SYLVIA. We're late.

BEX. Where's the milk?

SYLVIA. It's there.

BEX. Not got proper milk?

SYLVIA. Almond milk's better for you.

> *The mobile continues to ring.*

BEX. Tastes fucking rank.

SYLVIA. Excuse me?

BEX (*mumbles*). Sorry.

SYLVIA. Toast then?!

The mobile continues to ring.

BEX. I'm not hungry.

SYLVIA. Well you have to have something!

BEX. I just said I'm not hungry.

SYLVIA. But it's breakfast.

BEX. You can't make me / eat it.

SYLVIA. But breakfast is the most important meal of the day!

The mobile stops ringing. They stand there in silence for a moment. It's awkward.

Starting the day off shouting isn't good for anyone.

BEX. I'm not shouting. You're shouting.

SYLVIA. Last week you said almond milk would do.

BEX. Changed my mind. It's rank.

SYLVIA. Right. Well.

BEX. Don't wanna go school today. Feel sick.

SYLVIA. You're not sick.

BEX. I am. Got flu.

BEX coughs. SYLVIA's mobile starts to ring again.

SYLVIA. I haven't got time for this. You'll have to get the bus.

She takes out some money, gives it to BEX.

This isn't an opportunity to skive off again. I'll be ringing Miss Riley at lunch, check you made it in.

She goes to leave then turns back.

Are you sure you won't need a swimming costume?

BEX. It's not swimming.

SYLVIA. And don't forget your pack lunch, / it's in the fridge.

BEX. It's white-water rafting.

SYLVIA. I put you in two Babybels because…

BEX. Oh my god.

SYLVIA. Well just because…

The mobile continues to ring.

BEX. Are you not gonna get that?

SYLVIA *picks up the call on her mobile and leaves for work.* BEX *pours the Coco Pops in the bowl, adds the almond milk, takes one mouthful, chews, then spits it back out in disgust.*

BEX MEETS RUTH

Later that day.

A riverbank at Holme Pierrepont: the outdoor National Water Sports Centre. BEX *is stood looking out over the water sucking on a large fluorescent-green lollipop; deep in thought.* RUTH *is sat a few metres away reading the final Harry Potter book.*

BEX. I'm Bex. Bex Bentley. Like the car. Proper classy, that's me.

RUTH. I know who you are.

> RUTH *goes back to her book.* BEX *sucks on her lollipop. After a short while…*

BEX. Conversation's not your strong point is it? Can see why you're sat on your own reading Harry fucking Potter.

RUTH. Thalassophobia.

BEX. Is that some kind of Potter spell to make me fuck off?

RUTH. It's from the Greek word, thalassa, meaning sea. Fear of the sea. That's why I'm not taking part.

BEX. Um… but it's a river?

RUTH. Same thing.

BEX. Not really.

RUTH. One creates the other. You couldn't have a chicken without an egg.

BEX. So? Don't make a *chicken* an *egg* though, does it. Idiot.

> *Beat.*

> Oh my god. This girl right, she once found a chicken fetus when she cracked open an egg from a pack she bought from Beeston Tescos. A chicken fucking fetus. Yeah. Had these tiny little chicken legs all curled up like midget tyrannosaurus claws and some minging scraggy body that was sorta like snot. How cool is that? I think she was making scrambled eggs. She was all like 'ewww it's so gross' blah blah blah whatever, I'm like: fucking get over it, it's only a little chicken fetus, shove your scrambled egg in your gob and shut up.

> She's not my mate or anything. I read it in the *Mirror*.

RUTH. I'm vegan.

BEX. Oh. Why?

RUTH. I'm saving the planet from environmental catastrophe.

BEX. Maybe you're just going through a phase. I tried to be vegan once. On the first day I forgot and went to KFC.

Beat.

Miss Riley said I'm not allowed cos I can't swim.

First time anyone's ever paid for me to go on one of these school trips and she's telling me I've gotta sit on the bank and I can't take part, 'health and safety' bullshit. Get me in a raft. I'd be fine. I can handle myself.

RUTH. What happens if you fell in?

BEX. I dunno. Hold on or something. It's not fair.

Beat.

Do you know Dillon in the year above?

RUTH. Not personally no.

BEX. Has he got a girlfriend?

RUTH. I think he went out with Rachel Moore for a few weeks at some point, but to be honest, keeping up with gossip isn't exactly my forte.

BEX. I think he fancies me. Do you think people might like me more if I go out with him?

RUTH. Do people not like you?

BEX. Can I tell you a secret?

RUTH. I suppose.

BEX. You know on the bus here?

RUTH. Yeah...?

BEX. I was sat at the back cos I was tryna give Jamie Cragg a dead arm for calling me a homeless sket. And I was sat on top of him, right, pinning him down and he was proper squealing

like a little fat piggy, fucking – anyway, Miss Barker sent
Dillon to the back of the bus to break us up and Dillon took
Jamie by the collar, even though I was the one punching him,
and he practically threw Jamie into a seat a few rows down
and slyly came back and sat in Jamie's empty seat and. And.
Then. Well. Dillon was all like, 'Are you okay?... I haven't
seen you before.' And I was like proper getting so embarrassed
but also excited cos it's the first time since I started here that
anyone's actually asked me if I was okay, apart from the
teachers obviously but they don't really count cos they get
paid to ask don't they so that don't really mean shit. And then.
He stayed sat there. In Jamie's seat. Next to me. And every
time the bus driver went raggo round the corners Dillon's knee
would gently graze mine. And it sent these electric shocks all
up my spine and into my tummy like mad fireworks popping
off like 'bang', 'bang', 'bang' then like a little 'fizzzz'... and
my hand, my hand was just like sort of casually resting on my
leg and suddenly, out of nowhere – I mean we'd stopped
talking ages ago, I'd sort of muttered that I thought Jamie
Cragg was a little cunt and Dillon said 'takes one to know one'
and I just went red and smiled and did this sort of like stupid
laugh – but suddenly, all of a sudden, he just took my hand,
and held it into his, and sort of like, just sort of held my hand
in silence all of the rest of the way here. And don't laugh but.
Well in my head I swore that I would never let that hand hurt
anyone ever again.

RUTH. That's good then.

BEX. But.

RUTH. What?

BEX. He hasn't said anything to me since we arrived. Whatever.
I don't even care. I was hanging around the vending machines
hoping to catch him looking at me. I really felt like we had
this, this, moment. Like, connection thing. Are you sure he
hasn't got a girlfriend?

RUTH *shrugs then attempts to read her book.*

What's there to do round here then?

RUTH. Not much.

BEX. You gonna spend six weeks wanking over Harry Potter?

RUTH. –

BEX. Bet you fancy the ginger one.

RUTH. I don't.

BEX. Is my tongue green?

BEX *sticks her tongue out, reluctantly* RUTH *checks*.

RUTH. Yes.

BEX. Want one?

RUTH. No.

BEX. I'll check if it's alright for vegans?

RUTH *looks at* BEX.

RUTH. Dillon really isn't… Honestly I don't think you should bother.

BEX *offers her a lollipop*. RUTH *accepts it*.

I'm Ruth.

BEX IS NAUGHTY

Two days later.

Comprehensive school. DILLON *stands next to* BEX *outside the headteacher's office awaiting punishment, looking mischievous; desperately trying to whisper. They are both being watched by the secretary.*

DILLON. Your fault.

BEX. Wasn't.

DILLON. Was.

BEX. My hand slipped.

DILLON *smirks.*

DILLON. What were you in detention for anyways?

BEX. Mrs Knight caught me havin a fag behind music block. Bitch.

DILLON. Oooh. Rebel.

BEX. Oooh. Yeah. Whatever. Dick.

DILLON. You're gonna get suspended now.

BEX. You are.

DILLON. You are.

BEX. You started it.

DILLON. Such a liar!

BEX. Woulda got away with it if it weren't for your stupid cum face.

She does an impression of DILLON *having an orgasm. He looks a bit embarrassed.*

DILLON. As if.

BEX. Are you embarrassed?

DILLON. More like yours.

He does an impression of her.

BEX. You didn't make me cum.

DILLON. Whatever I wasn't even trying.

BEX. And anyway I don't look like that.

DILLON. How do you know?

BEX. I've practised.

DILLON. What?

BEX. In the mirror.

DILLON. Seriously?

BEX. I was curious.

DILLON. Yeah well it's different if you do it yourself.

An awkward silence.

BEX. Dillon... Is it true if you sit on your hand until it goes numb then wank yourself off it feels like someone else doing it?

DILLON *laughs, tries to hold it in.*

I'm asking you a serious question.

DILLON. I don't know do I. I ant never done it before.

BEX. Sure.

DILLON. I haven't.

BEX. Yeah.

DILLON. I haven't!

BEX. Yeah yeah sure I believe you.

DILLON. Oh fuck off.

BEX. Mardy bum.

DILLON. I'm not mardy fuck off.

BEX. Bet you do it as soon as you get home.

DILLON. Alright...

BEX. Will you?!

DILLON. If you want me to.

BEX. Will you think about me?

DILLON. Oh what.

BEX. Yeah but will ya though?

DILLON. Yeah. Maybe. Probably. Yeah. Fine I will.

They evade each other's gaze and smile. Their fingers touch.

BEX. Bet you're gonna be braggin bout this all week now. 'Blah blah blah Bex Bentley from Year 9 wanked me off in detention...' Loving it.

DILLON. I won't tell no one if you don't want me to.

BEX. Whatever. It's funny. It's a funny story. I'm gonna tell everyone.

DILLON. Alright then...

BEX. Wanna meet in detention tomorrow?

DILLON. No detention tomorrow. Last day of school.

BEX. Shame.

DILLON *smiles.*

DILLON. I gotta get a detention just to see you?

BEX. Maybe...

DILLON. Got plans for summer then or what?

BEX. Loads yeah.

DILLON. What you doing next week?

BEX. Depends.

DILLON. On what?

BEX. What you're offerin.

DILLON. Well. My dad's like got this caravan sorta thing in this field, go there, get pissed, have a barbecue, bonfire n that. Wi' my older brother. If you want to. Like, only if you want to... maybe you could –

SYLVIA *arrives in a fluster.* BEX *moves away from*
DILLON. *He looks at the ground.*

SYLVIA. Seriously Bex?

BEX. Didn't do nothin.

SYLVIA. They've already told me on the phone what you did.

BEX. Pure lies. Everybody hates me.

SYLVIA *looks* DILLON *up and down.*

SYLVIA (*to* DILLON). So is this the culprit?

BEX. Oh my god.

DILLON. Um.

Beat.

SYLVIA. And how old are you?

BEX. Don't answer / her.

SYLVIA. It's not a difficult question, / is it?

BEX. Sylvia.

DILLON. Fifteen.

BEX. He's only in the year above!

SLYVIA. Oh so you do know how old / she is then?!

BEX. Can you not do this / please?

SYLVIA (*to* BEX). So is he your boyfriend?

BEX. Stop!

SYLVIA. Well what. What is this?

DILLON. Oh. / Errrm.

BEX. It was my fucking idea alright!

SYLVIA. We'll talk about it at home.

BEX. Yay. Can't wait.

SYLVIA. You knew today was really important Bex. I had to leave the conference early.

BEX. So?

SYLVIA. How can I trust you home alone over summer?

BEX. You'll have to, won't / ya.

SYLVIA. I can't take any more time off work.

BEX. I'll be fine.

Beat.

Can entertain myself…

BEX *looks at* DILLON. DILLON *smirks.* SYLVIA *looks at* DILLON. *He looks back at the ground. The school bell rings.*

BEX WANTS TO PARTY

A week later. The start of the six weeks' holidays.

A caravan in the middle of a field off the A52. Music plays from inside. BEX *sits with sunglasses on her head, next to a barbecue with sausages cooking.* LEE *and* DILLON *are mid-play-fight,* DILLON *is trying to square up to* LEE. LEE *keeps advancing, like a mock-boxer, slapping* DILLON's *face gently.* LEE *pushes his chest hard and* DILLON *falls backwards onto the grass.* BEX *finds this hilarious.* DILLON *picks up a big chunk of wood and swings it towards* LEE, *it narrowly misses his head.* LEE *looks a bit shocked by this.* DILLON *is instantly filled with regret. There's a moment of tense stillness between the brothers as* LEE *towers over him. Suddenly* LEE *lurches forward and starts tickling* DILLON, *who squirms and squeals, begging him to stop. After a while* LEE *stops.* DILLON *gasps, out of breath.*

LEE. Did you fuckin see that?!

BEX. That was so close!

LEE. See how he tried to kill me?

BEX. That was literally like an inch away from your head!

DILLON. No it wasn't! Chatting / shit.

LEE. Oi! Don't intimidate the witness.

BEX. Yeah Dillon.

DILLON (*to* BEX). Can you stay for tea then?

LEE (*mocking* DILLON). 'Can you stay for / tea?'…

BEX. Dunno. What time / is it?

LEE (*to* DILLON). Get some buns then you little scrot.

DILLON. Them sausages smell like they're burning mate.

LEE. Y'not looking after our princess properly, she hasn't even got a beer! (*To* BEX.) Has he not offered you a beer?

BEX. I should get going actually.

LEE. Oh what! Was only just getting to know ya / duck!

BEX. I know… / sorry.

LEE. Must be able to tempt ya w'summit…

BEX. Nah / honest.

LEE. Got some WKD?

BEX. Thanks but.

LEE. Smirnoff?

BEX. I'm a bit late actually.

LEE. Stay for a sausage surely?

BEX. Probably got dinner waiting for me.

Beat.

DILLON. Could stop over next time if you want?

LEE. Oi oi.

DILLON. Nah not like that. Just meant / like.

BEX. Mmm… that's sweet yeah / but –

LEE. See, you've freaked her out now look.

BEX. Nah it's cool, it's just.

DILLON. I'll walk you home.

LEE. Ooooh. Romantic.

DILLON. Shut up.

LEE. Listen I might be a greedy fuck but I can't eat all these.
(*To* BEX.) Take a sausage for the walk.

BEX. Alright.

LEE. Get her a fucking bun then Dillon.

DILLON *disappears into the caravan.* LEE *stares at* BEX.

Ketchup or barbecue?

BEX. Ketchup. Obviously.

LEE. Good girl.

Beat.

He hasn't ever brought a girl back here before, you know. Must like you.

BEX. It's nice. I like it.

LEE. Your mum quite strict then?

BEX. Nah. She's not um. / She's not my –

LEE. It's alright. I get it. I would be with my daughter. If I had a daughter.

LEE *gives her a knowing smile.*

But you wanna party don't ya? Can see it in your eyes.

BEX. Might do... Yeah.

LEE. Well then. Next time. Tell her you're sleeping at a mate's.

SYLVIA LOVES BEX

A couple of weeks later. Early August.

SYLVIA*'s kitchen.* SYLVIA *is stood by the table.* BEX *is stood at the back door in her Parka, drenched. Two police officers have just left. The kettle is boiling slowly. A long silence, it's awkward…*

SYLVIA. Do you want to take your coat off?

BEX. No.

SYLVIA. You're soaking.

BEX. So?

SYLVIA. But you'll / catch a dreadful cold…

BEX. Get on with it then.

SYLVIA. Excuse me?

BEX. Bollock me then.

SYLVIA. I'm not going to [bollock you] – Please, Bex, can you just take your coat off?

BEX. Fucksake. Fine. God.

> BEX *takes her coat off and throws it onto the floor. The kettle finishes boiling.* SYLVIA *pours the water into two cups.*

Can I go now?

SYLVIA. I'm making you a cup of tea.

BEX. Did you ask me if I wanted one?

SYLVIA. I just thought.

BEX. Are you gonna force me to drink it?

SYLVIA. No but.

BEX. Cos that's rape that is.

SYLVIA. What?

BEX. There's this cartoon that were on Snapchat about making a cup of tea. And it's like. You ask someone if they want a cup of tea. And they're like, 'hmm I dunno if I want a cup of tea' or whatever and then you make them the cup of tea anyway and then they say 'oh actually I don't really want a cup of tea' and then you still make them drink the cup of tea and then basically that's the same as rape. Or something. Or. Like you wouldn't make an unconscious person drink a cup of tea would you?

SYLVIA. Hmmm… No I / probably –

BEX. And you didn't even ASK me if I even wanted the tea in the first place so.

SYLVIA. Maybe this is something I have to watch to – sorry, I still don't fully understand how we went from tea to rape.

BEX. I hate you. You're not even listening to me.

SYLVIA. I don't have Snapchat.

Silence.

Do you. I mean. Well. Do you want to drink the tea or? I've made it now so…

BEX. That's the whole fucking point of the thing?! Just cos you've made it doesn't mean I HAVE to drink it!

SYLVIA. Okay. Fair enough. I'll just.

BEX. Oh fine! I'll drink the fucking tea.

BEX *takes the tea from* SYLVIA.

Happy now?

An awkward beat.

SYLVIA. I'm not angry with you.

BEX. Don't care.

SYLVIA. Just, if you think I'm angry or something, I want you to know, I'm not.

BEX. You called the police?

SYLVIA. Yes, I feel a bit silly about that now.

BEX. Social's gonna be proper on my case now. Cheers.

SYLVIA. I'll tell Tracey / it was my –

BEX. She's gonna give me the 'trust is a two-way street' chat.

SYLVIA. I'll explain to Tracey I might have overreacted.

BEX. You're a nutjob.

SYLVIA. I can see how it may seem that way.

BEX. Was only gone for one night really.

SYLVIA. I was worried about you.

BEX. Well I'm fine aren't I.

An awkward beat.

SYLVIA. Tracey will need to meet them. This family.

BEX. –

SYLVIA. You know the procedure.

BEX. Yeah. I know.

SYLVIA. She'll be questioning me, how I let this happen. You do realise that?

Beat.

Were you with that boy?

BEX. No!

SYLVIA. Bex.

BEX. I was at a fuckin sleepover!

SYLVIA. Really?

BEX. I weren't exactly out on a mad one!

SYLVIA. Just tell me the truth.

BEX. She's a proper geek. She likes wizards. And *Doctor Who*. And weird singers from the eighties that wear loads of make-up even though they're blokes.

SYLVIA. Oh. Well she sounds nice.

BEX. Yeah. She is.

SYLVIA. But if you *were* with that boy / I'd rather –

BEX. I'm telling the fuckin truth!

SYLVIA. Okay, okay!

Beat.

I would have probably let you go, if you'd asked.

BEX. Oh. God. Well. I didn't, did I so. What the fuck do you want me to say? I'm sorry! I'm fucking sorry! Whatever. I hate you.

SYLVIA. You could just phone me next time, tell / me where –

BEX. Oh right. Shall I phone you like every hour, when I'm on the bog like 'Sylvia I'm alright', or when I'm down Co-op like 'Sylvia I'm not dead'. Is that what you want? You're a bit high-maintenance, bit needy, anyone ever told you that before?

SYLVIA. It comes from a good place.

BEX. What did you think was gonna happen to me?

SYLVIA. I didn't know where you were. I was worried. I'm your mum. I'm allowed to worry.

BEX. Apart from you're not my mum.

SYLVIA. No, sorry. Not your. Sorry. What would. What do you want to call me?

BEX. Sylvia. That's your name isn't it?

SYLVIA. Well. I'm Sylvia. And I worry about you as Sylvia. I'm not trying to be. Needy. Or hard work. I just. I know it hasn't been long but I suppose what it is, is that… I mean, you've done this before. And maybe for you it's not. Not that it's not. But perhaps it doesn't mean as much or. No. I'm not trying to tell you what this means to you, sorry, I don't know what I mean to you, not just me, this, anyway, what am I saying? What I'm saying is. What I'm saying is. Look what I'm saying is. I worry. Sometimes. Not all the time. Just a healthy, normal amount that a mother, or someone who is sort of like a mother, should do. That's. Well yeah, that's it.

An awkward silence.

BEX. She made me watch *QI* for fucksake.

SYLVIA. *QI*...?

BEX. Yeah! They were talking about some dog called
   Esmeralda who was the first thing to get a boob job. They
   like tested on it or something, until it chewed the stitches and
   they fell out. Ruth was banging on about animal cruelty,
   same hippy shit like what you say, and I was just making her
   and her dad laugh by sticking socks down my bra, crawling
   around doing a dumb impression of this dog with tits.
   Woofing and licking him and shit. I think she likes me.

SYLVIA. You could invite her here if you like? It's good that
   you've made a friend.

BEX. Make me sound like such a loser.

SYLVIA. You're not a loser Bex. I'm sure you're really cool.

BEX. Oh great. Well. If you think I'm cool I'm probably
   fucked.

SYLVIA. Oh. No. Um... So it's just Ruth and...

BEX. Her mum and dad.

SYLVIA. Oh right, nice.

BEX. Yeah. Her mum cooked this vegetable thing called ray-gu
   that was minging. But I'll probably go round there again.
   Her dad even offered me a lift home because it was raining
   but I felt bad so I told him I had money for the bus. I didn't.
   Took me like three hours to walk home.

   Beat.

   Alright that's an exaggeration. It was about forty-five minutes
   but it is proper raining. But I bet he'll give me a lift next time.
   So. If I'm not here. And I'm not at the park. And I'm not down
   Co-op. Then I'll probably be at Ruth's so don't go all skitzo
   crazy bitch on me and call the police again alright?

SYLVIA. Only if you promise to always tell me where you're
   going. Just a text.

BEX. God. Alright. Deal.

SYLVIA. I really am awfully fond of you.

An awkward beat.

BEX. Right. Well this is awkward now.

SYLVIA. Sorry.

BEX LOVES SYLVIA

A week later, one evening.

BEX*'s bedroom.* BEX *and* RUTH *stare at* SYLVIA, *who's awkwardly wearing a pink cardigan and pearls.*

BEX. Where's he taking ya, Bible club?

SYLVIA. I was going for the smart-casual look.

RUTH. The pearls look cute.

BEX. First outfit. Definitely.

RUTH. Mmm.

SYLVIA. Sure?

   The girls nod in unison. SYLVIA *leaves.*

BEX. What you on about, the pearls looked shit.

RUTH. Some people need positive encouragement.

BEX. Facts are facts.

RUTH. Dating must be scary when you're old.

BEX. Yeah. It's shit. Imagine being Sylvia's age and you STILL didn't have a boyfriend.

   RUTH *gets some books out of her bag.*

   I could see you ending up like Sylvia.

RUTH. And why is that a bad thing?

BEX. Have you really never kissed anyone? Like literally not one boy?

RUTH. No.

BEX. Are you a lesbian?

RUTH. No?

BEX. Do you fancy me? It's okay if you do. Most people probably do.

RUTH. No.

BEX. Are you saving your virginity for David Tennant?

RUTH. No!

BEX. Because I hate to have to be the one to break it to you Ruth, but I don't think it's gonna happen mate.

RUTH. Shut up.

BEX. Don't cry about it.

RUTH. Just because I'm not like you doesn't mean I'm weird.

BEX. That's not what I'm sayin. We both know I'm the freak.

RUTH. No one's perfect.

BEX. My nipples are. Dillon said so.

RUTH. You showed him your nipples?

BEX. Erm, he's not got special X-ray vision duh-brain. This ain't *Doctor Who* world now Ruth. It's real life.

RUTH. Did you… sleep over… when you went to the party?

BEX. Obviously. Got absolutely shitfaced. Took a pill. Like ecstasy. Like an ecstasy pill.

RUTH. Really?

BEX. Oh my god it was so funny. I was just like sick everywhere. It was amazing.

RUTH. Right, cool…

BEX. Told Sylvia I was sleeping over at yours, if she asks or whatever. So don't be a little skank and drop me in it.

RUTH. I wouldn't.

BEX. His brother is so joke. And his dad. They let me do whatever I want. His dad said I'm basically like the daughter he never had / so.

RUTH. Bex did you and Dillon… like, have sex?

BEX. Eww no! I'm making him work for it! Got him to buy me a pack of Tangfastics and a can of Lilt before I showed him my tits.

RUTH. At least you've got tits.

BEX. Awww. Ruth. Don't. You're pretty. Someone will love you.

RUTH. They don't love you. They just love your tits.

BEX. Same thing.

RUTH. Not really.

> *Beat.* RUTH *is poised with a book in her hand.*
>
> Okay. So.

BEX. I don't do reading. I told ya.

RUTH. Let me just read you the blurb it might draw you in.

BEX. –

RUTH. They're not soppy love stories or anything.

BEX. What if I can't read it all the way to the end?

RUTH. What if you just try?

BEX. Alright Hitler.

RUTH. I just think you might be pleasantly surprised.

> BEX *reads the back of a book.*

BEX. Evil dolls and shit?

RUTH. Oh that one's great. It's set in this house with this girl who has to fight these evil-doll spirits that possess her mum and in the end she's left all alone cos they make the mum kill herself and –

> Sorry.

BEX. For what?

RUTH. Nothing. I just should have. Thought. Sorry.

BEX. Blah blah blah evil dolls whatever. I'll take this one.

RUTH. Are you sure?

> SYLVIA *appears at the bedroom door dressed in a different outfit, looking nervous.*

SYLVIA. This one?

BEX. Oh yeah.

RUTH. You do look great.

SYLVIA. Thank you Ruth.

BEX. You almost look sexy.

Beat.

You are gonna put some make-up on though, right?

SYLVIA. Oh. I was just. I mean…

BEX. Sylvia. Sweetheart.

SYLVIA. I haven't got long.

BEX *gets her make-up from her bag and begins to display them like a beauty counter.*

BEX. Perfection takes time. He can wait.

SYLVIA. I prefer a more natural look.

BEX. Trust me. I've got a vision.

SYLVIA. I really don't have much time.

BEX. It's your birthday Sylvia. Relax. You're meant to be fashionably late anyways. It will make him want you more.

SYLVIA. Will it?

BEX. Did you use that cream I got you?

SYLVIA. Oh. Um. No I / haven't.

BEX. Ruth. Get it for me please.

SYLVIA. It's in my bedroom on my dresser.

BEX. The one for ageing skin.

RUTH. On it.

RUTH *exits on a mission.*

BEX. You best not get murdered on your birthday.

SYLVIA. I'll try not to.

BEX. He's literally a stranger. He could be a murderer.

SYLVIA. Perhaps this isn't a good idea.

BEX. You'll be fab. Just don't talk too much about your cats.
Or me.

SYLVIA. I could rearrange it. I should be spending my birthday
with you.

BEX. Oi don't use me as an excuse!

SYLVIA. I'm not.

BEX. You got a lot to offer the world. Like you're genuinely
a nice person. And you're actually really beautiful, you
know, in an older-lady kind of way.

SYLVIA. Why are you being so nice to me?

BEX. I can be nice. Sit down.

SYLVIA *sits*.

On a level though. I do think you're really brave for doing this.

SYLVIA. How so?

BEX. Like I hope this date goes well because…

SYLVIA. Because what?

BEX. Because you act like everything's all cool n that, and like
you're some independent woman and all that shit but. Really.
Underneath it all. I can see how lonely you are.

RUTH *enters with the cream, mission complete*.

RUTH. Ta-dah!!

BEX. Brian is in for a fucking treat!

SYLVIA *smiles but quietly looks wounded*.

BEX'S HEART BREAKS

Two weeks later. The last week of the summer holidays.

SYLVIA's kitchen. A letter is on the table. Smashed plates are on the floor. They are midway through an argument. BEX is wild with anger.

BEX. Why did you tell that / bitch?!

SYLVIA. I should have told you. But I wanted to wait until they sent that, till it was in writing, until I'd heard / from Tracey and –

BEX. You're so fucking stupid!

SYLVIA. Until they said it was a definite and. Bex it's not Tracey's fault. She's trying to do her best for you, / she really cares about –

BEX. Talking about me behind my back, / with that cow!

SYLVIA. No! I had / to!

BEX. Since when?

SYLVIA. Oh I don't know… some time around my birthday –

BEX. Your birthday? Seriously?

SYLVIA. Well I've been / feeling –

BEX. I saved up my pocket money the whole fucking summer so I could buy you that present from Boots, you ungrateful / cow!

SYLVIA. Oh god, Jesus, I loved it, / I really –

BEX. Ring her then! Tell your best mate Trace to come / get me. Go on.

SYLVIA. Bex. Please just listen to me –

BEX. Go back to your sad little life alone with your stinky shitty cats. I hope *YOU* fucking kill yourself / n all!

SYLVIA. I wanted to tell you I did. Honestly Bex, I've been torn in half, racked with guilt. The other day I had to go to the loo just to take five minutes to sit on the toilet and cry, just thinking about you, just thinking about / what –

BEX. Stop making this all about you!

SYLVIA. I'm not! I'm just trying to make you understand how difficult this is for me! Not this. / Not us but –

BEX. Fuck it off then! Leave me then! If I'm so / fucking difficult.

SYLVIA. Leaving you is difficult! I don't want to leave you! They assess me. My mental health. They don't think I'm fit to look after you any more!

BEX. I FUCKING HATE YOU!

Beat.

SYLVIA. You don't.

BEX. I do!

SYLVIA. You don't. I know you don't. / I can feel it. You can scream in my face all you want but. I can. I can feel it Bex. And that's okay. It's okay, it's okay…

BEX. I HATE YOU! I hate you! I hate you! I hate you! I hate you. I hate you. I hate you. I hate you. I hate you. I hate you. I hate you. I hate you. I hate you. I hate you…

BEX *breaks down.*

A long silence.

Stillness.

SYLVIA. Look at me…? Bex, look at me please. Please… Please Bex? No? Okay. Okay fine. I just. I just want you to know that. You're so fucking special.

BEX. I'm not.

SYLVIA. You are.

BEX. I'm really not.

SYLVIA. I promise / you –

BEX. If I'm so special, then why does everybody leave?

Beat.

SYLVIA. None of this. What I'm going through right now, what
   I'm putting you through, none of this is your fault. I swear to
   you. What we had, what we have is... I feel it. It feels. I can
   feel you care. I mean, maybe not a moment ago but. Even
   then actually. Because I know the reason why you're angry
   is because... this is hard. I really think you do care, in your
   own unique way. Maybe. I don't know.

Silence.

It's like... I'm a carrot. Okay. In the fridge. This is what it's
like. I'm a carrot in the fridge.

BEX *looks at* SYLVIA.

No don't give me that look. I'm. I'm. I'm being serious. I'm
trying to. It's like I'm a carrot. In the fridge and. Because if
you think about it. When the door's closed. It's very dark.
And there's no air. And it's very cold. And it's very lonely –
there's no other food in the fridge. And this carrot. Me. I'm
the carrot. Is... Well / I'm –

BEX. I'm not five fucking years old.

SYLVIA. Oh. No. I just –

BEX. I know what depression is.

SYLVIA. Oh. Yes. God. I'm / so –

BEX. If you say sorry one more time I swear on my mum's
   grave I'll punch you in the face.

SYLVIA. Fair enough.

Beat.

When I think about you my chest feels like it's about to
explode and this energy pulses through me, heat, rising all
the way up through my veins from my heart.

It's. Powerful. Truly.

They look into each other's soul. For a long time. Then BEX
hugs SYLVIA *and begins to cry in her arms.* SYLVIA *kisses
her head.*

BEX DANCES ALONE

A week later. The end of the six weeks' holidays.

Night. The caravan is lit up. Music plays from inside, really loud this time. BEX *is alone dancing, she looks off her face.* DILLON *opens the door to the caravan and stands watching her for a bit, swigging on a bottle of vodka. He approaches* BEX, *pours some vodka into her mouth. They kiss.*

LEE *moves a curtain in the caravan to one side and stares out at them through the window.*

BEX IS GOING TO A PARTY

A week later. Friday night after school.

RUTH*'s bedroom. A sexy R&B song plays loud from* BEX*'s mobile.* BEX *grinds in front of the mirror, singing and swigging from a little bottle of rum. She's really going for it.* RUTH *is sat on her bed with her laptop open, looking at social media.*

RUTH. Have you seen this Bex? On Dillon's account. Bex. Bex! Can you turn it down?

> BEX *rolls her eyes and turns it down.*

BEX. What?

RUTH. Sorry. You couldn't hear me.

> BEX *poses in the mirror, applying make-up.* RUTH *stares at her.*

> Is Dillon your boyfriend now?

BEX. Why?

RUTH. He doesn't really speak to you at school.

BEX. He's in the year above. We barely see each other.

RUTH. So you've forgiven him. For the whole. Video thing.

BEX. Oh my god. That was like so last week.

RUTH. Have you seen his status?

BEX. No one's even talking about it / any more.

RUTH. They are… Online they are.

BEX. Does this skirt look too slutty?

> RUTH *rolls her eyes.*

> You were meant to be helping me get ready!

RUTH. Oh yeah, great.

BEX. Why you being mardy for?

RUTH. I don't really care. I'm not coming to the party am I.

BEX. You don't even like Dillon. You like reading and homework.

BEX *turns the music back up.* RUTH *opens her school bag and takes a revision book out.*

RUTH. I've actually got some English I should be doing so…

BEX *pauses the track.*

BEX. It's not really a party otherwise I'd invite you.

RUTH. It's fine.

BEX. It's just Dillon and his brother.

RUTH. Whatever.

BEX. What the fuck have I done wrong?

RUTH. You're acting as if nothing's happened. Like everything's cool. Like you're just going to go there tonight and it will probably happen all over again.

BEX. He is basically my boyfriend Ruth!

RUTH. The whole school has seen it.

BEX. Don't care. Everyone thought I looked hot so.

RUTH. Why would you let him film you… you know.

BEX. You can say it out loud Ruth.

RUTH. You know…

BEX. Scared your dad might hear?

RUTH. Sucking him off.

BEX *laughs.*

BEX. Oh my god you're such a virgin.

RUTH. So are you.

BEX. Whatever.

Beat.

RUTH. You can sleep here. If you don't wanna go back to the care home. If that's why you go to the caravan. / You can –

BEX. I'm going because I have fun. They're my friends.

RUTH. I'm just saying you can sleep over here if you want to.

BEX. Well I don't want to.

RUTH. Fine. Go do whatever with Dillon. Just don't cry about it to me when he acts like a dick again.

BEX. When have I EVER cried in front of you? Bitch.

RUTH leaves. BEX sits on the bed, opens up the laptop and reads some of the messages. She slams the laptop shut and swigs the rum.

MARK (*off*). Bex?

She quickly shoves the bottle back into her bag. MARK, RUTH's dad, appears at the door, he smiles. BEX evades his gaze.

Have you two had a fall-out?

BEX. No.

Beat.

MARK. Gonna watch *Jurassic Park* after dinner, if you fancy it?

Beat.

Ruth told me things didn't work out with Sylvia…

BEX. –

MARK. Such a shame.

BEX. Yeah well… Basically she was an absolute nutter. Like. Yeah like all this dodgy shit came out. Tracey wouldn't tell me all about it but. From what I gathered she used to be some sort of paedo-nun or something.

MARK. Sylvia? A paedo-nun?

BEX. I know right.

MARK. But I thought she was a Buddhist?

BEX. Quiet ones innit.

Beat.

MARK. Are you okay?

BEX. Where's Carol?

MARK. Oh she's staying at her mum's for a bit. Work stuff.

BEX. Ruth said you're having a divorce.

MARK. Did she?

BEX. Are you? Or did you kill her?

MARK. No, I um… definitely / haven't –

BEX. She must have had great tits before she had Ruth for you to wanna shag her.

MARK. Hey, come on.

BEX. Sorry but she was a mardy cow and a crap cook.

MARK. Oi. Her pasta bake weren't too bad.

BEX. She was like so beige. Like nothingness. Like I've probably got more personality in my little toe than her. She was like boiled cabbage.

MARK. Alright, that's enough now.

   BEX *smiles at* MARK.

   Can I ask you something…

BEX. Yeah.

MARK. You'll tell me the truth?

BEX. Obviously.

MARK. Are you drinking alcohol in my house?

BEX. What? No?

MARK. Bex…

BEX. I wouldn't!

MARK. Come on I'm not / an idiot..

BEX. What has she said t'ya?

MARK. I saw it earlier, in your bag.

BEX. It's not mine, it's for a mate, I was meant to be going to a party.

MARK. A party? Where?

BEX. Not with Ruth or anything. I wasn't getting her into trouble or whatever.

MARK. Well I'd prefer you not to drink it while you're here.

BEX. I do respect you, okay?

MARK. Okay.

BEX. I respect you. And this house, a lot. Like. A lot. Okay?

MARK. Okay.

Beat.

Will you need dropping at this party?

BEX. Nah. It's fine. It's not far.

RUTH *appears at the bedroom door unseen.*

MARK. Well you're welcome to stay if you want.

BEX. Thanks but…

MARK. You'll always have a home here. Know that right?

BEX. Really?

RUTH. Mum's on the phone. She wants to speak to you.

MARK. Oh. Joy.

MARK *smiles at* BEX *before he exits.* RUTH *stands near the doorway awkwardly.*

BEX. Finish the homework already?

RUTH. Not yet.

BEX. Sorry for calling you a bitch.

RUTH. Did you decide on your outfit then?

BEX IS RESCUED

Later that night. The caravan.

Loud music. BEX *staggers out of the caravan into the cold wearing only her bra and pants.* LEE*'s voice can be heard from inside the caravan, laughing, and the odd phrase; 'little slag', 'proper tight', etc.* BEX *is clutching her mobile phone, attempting to read a text message. Suddenly it rings. She answers it…*

BEX. Ruth listen to me. No don't! I didn't want you to tell him! I can walk. I'm walking. Ruth, I'm walking! I'm –

She falls face down in the grass.

Fuck.

The caravan door opens and DILLON *appears, he slams it behind him.*

DILLON. What just happened in there? In the bedroom.

BEX. I need to go. / Home.

DILLON. Are you still mad at me about / the video?

BEX. Can you. Get my stuff.

DILLON. Bex…

BEX. Please / Dillon.

DILLON. Did you just fuck my brother?

BEX. I really. Need. / To –

DILLON. Bex what just happened in the bedroom?

Beat.

Take my coat you twat, it's freezin.

He chucks his coat at her.

BEX. Am I your girlfriend?

DILLON. Do you fancy Lee is that it?

BEX. I wanted to lose my virginity to you. We haven't / even [had sex].

DILLON. I get it if you do. He's older n / that.

BEX. I don't / Dillon.

DILLON. We shoulda never played dares. Always push it too far. Winding me / up.

BEX. Do you hate me now?

DILLON. It's cos he knows I like you. Fucking winding me up, right? Weren't ya? Cos you wouldn't do that to me, would ya? Cos it proper sounded like. Like. But it wasn't was it? You were both just winding me up. Thinking you're fucking funny. You didn't… He didn't actually. He wouldn't…

Silence.

I was tryna open the bedroom door, swear.

BEX. I know.

DILLON. I was banging on the door…

They sit in silence for a moment. He holds BEX's *hand.*

BEX. Do you remember when we first met? At the back of the bus.

DILLON *looks at* BEX.

You punched Jamie Cragg. No. I punched Jamie Cragg.

You saved me because. You held my hand. All the way there. You held my hand. And you didn't even need to say anything. You just knew. You held my hand and you just knew.

DILLON. I don't remember.

BEX. On the bus.

LEE (*inside the caravan*). Oi I thought this was meana be a party?!

BEX. I'm not going back in there Dillon.

DILLON. I'll tell him you don't want to.

BEX. Please Dillon. I can't. I. Oh fuck. I –

BEX *suddenly throws up on herself.*

DILLON. Oh what.

LEE *pops his head out of the caravan and looks at the scene.*

LEE. What she playin at yoof?!

DILLON. She don't wanna come in there Lee, she's. She's too mashed. She just chucked up on herself.

LEE. Pull yourself together duck!

DILLON. Get her some water or summit.

LEE. Urr she fuckin stinks!

LEE *goes back into the caravan.* BEX *throws up again.* DILLON *rubs her back.*

DILLON. It's okay. Get it all out.

LEE *comes back with a washing-up bowl full of water and pours it over* BEX*'s head.*

LEE. Here y'are love.

She winces, it's cold.

DILLON. What the / fuck.

LEE. What? Water innit?... Come then babe.

LEE *yanks* BEX*'s arm till she's stood swaying.*

Gonna get these off ya cos you stink of your own sick darlin, okay?

LEE *starts to take off her bra and pants.* BEX *is attempting to cover herself, she flinches at his hands on her bare skin.* DILLON *stares at his brother touching* BEX.

DILLON. Lee.

LEE. What? Dad won't want her stinkin the caravan out.

DILLON. I'll put her in the shower.

LEE. Cheap as fuck underwear anyway. Chuck em away innit.

Suddenly a pair of headlights blinds the boys as a car haphazardly pulls up next to the caravan.

Who the fuck is this?

DILLON. Is it the police?

LEE. Not the police you twat.

MARK *gets out of the car. Followed by* RUTH.

MARK. Oi.

LEE. Is it her dad?

DILLON. She ain't got / a dad.

MARK. Take your hands off her!

LEE. Who the fuck are you?

RUTH. Dad don't!

DILLON. Ruth?!

MARK (*to* RUTH). Get back in / the car.

DILLON. What you doing here?

MARK. I'm taking her home.

LEE. Fucking take her. I don't want her.

LEE *pushes* BEX *towards* MARK.

DILLON. Was tryna look after her Ruth / I promise.

LEE. She ain't worth it son.

LEE *grabs* DILLON *by the collar and yanks him into the caravan.* MARK *takes off his jacket and puts it around* BEX.

RUTH. Bex are you okay?

BEX. Fucksake / Ruth!

MARK. Calm it.

BEX. I said I could / walk!

MARK. In the car. / Now.

BEX. Don't touch me, / I'm fucking fine!

MARK. Alright, / alright.

BEX. Why the fuck did / you –

MARK. Enough of the / language!

RUTH. You rang me! / You said –

BEX. You shouldn't be here!

RUTH. I'm sorry! / I thought –

MARK. Just get in the car!

BEX CAN'T SLEEP

Later that night.

MARK*'s living room. He is sat watching the television alone in the dark, drinking a bottle of Peroni. The door creaks open.* BEX *is stood behind it in some pyjamas.* MARK *jumps.*

MARK. Jesus.

BEX. I can't sleep. Can I. Can I come in, please?

MARK. Course.

Silence.

Sit down then.

She sits next to him. He swigs his beer. After a while…

Go there a lot for parties, do ya?

BEX. Not really.

MARK. How do you know them?

BEX. School.

MARK. He looked a bit old to be at school.

BEX. Nothing happened.

MARK. Where you living at the moment?

BEX. Why?

MARK. I'll drop you off in the morning.

BEX. I can get the bus.

MARK. I'm dropping you off. Make sure you're safe.

An awkward beat.

You with a new family?

BEX. Care home in town. Nearly sent me to Wales.

MARK. Wales?

BEX. Looked dead beautiful actually. I googled it but. Told Tracey I didn't wanna leave here so.

MARK. Well that's nice of her then, to let you stay.

BEX. It weren't cos I asked. Cos of my GCSEs. All that crap. Said it's best if I stay put.

MARK. Whereabouts is it? The care home.

BEX. On the big roundabout, near the shopping centre.

MARK. You like it there then?

　　BEX *shrugs*.

　　Did you tell them you were going to this party?

BEX. Sort of.

MARK. You can't let yourself get in that state Bex.

BEX. I've drank more than that before.

MARK. That's not the point.

　　Beat.

　　I'm gonna have to tell someone what happened.

BEX. Don't.

MARK. Why were you... What would have happened if I didn't turn up?

BEX. Suppose it weren't my most graceful tactical chunder ever but –

MARK. You could barely walk.

BEX. Was about to give me a shower. Take me / to –

MARK. A shower?

BEX. I just needed a lie-down. Look at me. I'm fine.

MARK. Something wasn't... / [right].

BEX. You're being so dramatic.

MARK. I should tell someone. I should tell Tracey.

BEX. If you tell Tracey she'll bollock me and then I won't be allowed to come here any more. Please don't.

MARK. But…

BEX. I like coming here.

MARK. Are you sure / you're… [alright?]

BEX. I'm fine. Swear down.

MARK. It's really late. You / should –

BEX. Not tired.

They both sit there, unsure what to say.

MARK. Made me jump.

BEX. Did I?

MARK. Yeah. Creeping about.

BEX. Was worried I might walk in on you having a wank.

MARK. What?

BEX. Cos that would be like so awkward, wouldn't it?

MARK. That's not funny.

BEX. I know you probably have.

MARK. Have what?

BEX. Wanked about me.

MARK. I haven't. I'm / not a –

BEX. I'm not a kid.

MARK. You are.

BEX. You know I'm not.

MARK. Yes. You are. / You're –

BEX. I'm fucking not. I'm nearly fifteen.

MARK. You should be in bed. Get to bed. Now.

BEX. I like it when you tell me off.

MARK. I'm not telling you off.

Beat.

BEX. Why can't *you* sleep?

MARK. What do you think Ruth would say if she saw you like this, / with me?

BEX. Thinking about Cabbage Carol?

MARK. No.

BEX. Do you miss her?

MARK. No.

BEX. Bet you haven't had sex in months.

MARK. This is the last time I'm gonna ask you now Bex. Go to bed.

BEX *looks a little hurt.*

BEX. Mark…

MARK. What?

BEX. Nothing.

Beat.

MARK. Why can't you sleep?

BEX. I was just thinking, about stuff.

A dark cloud hangs in the air between them.

MARK.…Bad stuff?

BEX. Mm. No. Not.

MARK. I do think it's best to tell someone.

BEX. No, it's just…

MARK. What? What is it then?

BEX. Doesn't matter.

MARK. It does matter. If you can't sleep.

BEX. Nah. It's silly. It's.

MARK. I know I'm not. I mean I'm not your… It's not my place to stop you doing whatever you're gonna do but. If you need me. You know, need someone, if you ever find yourself in a sticky situation or you're scared. You can call me. You know that right?

BEX *blushes*.

BEX. Yeah.

A tense silence. BEX *stares at him,* MARK *smiles and shakes his head.*

MARK. You've been good for Ruth. I was worried about her. She doesn't... talk to me much. How is she doing? All the stuff with me and her / mum...

BEX. She's alright. Ruth's always alright.

MARK. You two are funny.

BEX. Why?

MARK. Cos you're so... Well, she's like... And you're like...

BEX. I'm like what?

MARK. I don't know.

BEX. Go on...

Beat.

What do you think about me?

MARK. What do you mean?

BEX. Just sometimes... I wonder what you think of me.

MARK. Good things.

BEX. Good things?

MARK. You got a beautiful soul Bex.

BEX. Beautiful?

MARK. Sorry. That was. I just mean.

BEX. No. That's. It's nice. I don't think I've ever been called beautiful before. By a boy. A man. A. Whatever.

MARK. You shouldn't need a man to tell you you're beautiful Bex. You should just know it. In here.

He touches BEX*'s chest just above her heart.*

BEX. I'm really not.

MARK. You just don't realise it.

BEX. Do you really think so?

MARK *places his hand on her knee.*

MARK. You are. You're beautiful.

BEX DOESN'T WANT TO PARTY

The following Friday.

BEX *is waiting at the school gates listening to music on some headphones.* DILLON *approaches from behind her.*

DILLON. Alright?

> BEX *doesn't hear him.*

> Bex?

> *He tentatively pokes* BEX*'s shoulder, she jumps, pulls a headphone out.*

BEX. What you playing at? / Dick.

DILLON. Sorry. I said 'you alright'. You didn't hear me.

> *An awkward beat.*

> You waiting for someone?

BEX. None of your business.

DILLON. Is it a guy or something?

BEX. What do you want Dillon?

DILLON. Oh. Um. Dunno.

BEX. Well then.

DILLON. Give you a hug or summit? Been avoiding me all week.

BEX. Haven't.

DILLON. Are you mad at me?

> BEX *shakes her head.*

> Can I have a hug then?

> BEX *looks at him then wraps her arms around his waist.*

> I told Miss Knight to suck my dick so I got a detention. Thought maybe you'd be there.

BEX. Idiot.

DILLON. I was working at the weekend. Made a bit of money.

BEX.... And?

DILLON. Thought maybe I could take you on a date. Like. Proper. If you want?

BEX. Where?

DILLON. Nando's or summit. Or Chinese buffet? All-you-can-eat in town? It's proper peng and you can eat as many duck spring rolls as you want.

BEX. I don't like Chinese.

DILLON. Where do you wanna go then?

BEX. Somewhere posh.

DILLON. Posh?!

BEX. Yeah like Pizza Express.

DILLON. Alright. I could wear my shirt.

BEX. Your school shirt?

DILLON. Nah, nah, I've got a proper shirt. For weddings and funerals n that.

BEX. You're paying.

DILLON. Obviously.

BEX *smiles at* DILLON.

Got the caravan to myself tomorrow night too. Lee's in Amsterdam for his thirtieth birthday so...

RUTH *appears behind them both, she hovers.*

I want you to be my girlfriend.

BEX. Just us two?

DILLON. Just us two. (*To* RUTH.) Y'alright?

RUTH *half-smiles and nods her head.*

BEX (*to* RUTH). You nearly made me late for my bus.

RUTH. Sorry.

> BEX *takes out a book from her bag, hands it to* RUTH.

Do you think we could talk?

BEX. Haven't really got anything to say to ya.

RUTH. I told you I'm sorry.

BEX. Yeah well.

RUTH. Could come round for tea if you want? My dad's cooking lasagne.

BEX. Get. The fucking. Message Ruth. I just don't think we should be friends any more.

RUTH. But…

> LEE *appears behind the girls.*

BEX (*to* DILLON). See you tomorrow night then.

DILLON. Tomorrow night. Can't wait.

> BEX *and* DILLON *kiss.*

LEE. Tomorrow night yeah, what you sayin!

BEX (*to* DILLON). I'll ring you later.

LEE. Rude. Not sayin hello to me or what.

BEX. I'm late for the bus.

LEE. Be another one in a minute. Chill out! Gimme a fuckin hug then! Man's birthday tomorrow innit! We're all friends aren't we?

> BEX *reluctantly gives* LEE *a hug. He playfully scruffs up her hair.*

DILLON. But wait, I thought you / were –

LEE. The lads 'ave proper messed me about this weekend Dillon! Lost the money for the flights, hotel deposit, everything! Proper had my sights set on destroyin some birds in the red-light district n all! Pussy and gear on tap. Are ya mad?! Woulda been fucking heaven mate. The pricks.

LEE *clocks* RUTH.

(*To* RUTH.) Sorry duck, these twats don't know manners if it smacked em in the face! I'm Lee. I'm Dillon's older / brother.

RUTH. Brother. Yeah. I know.

LEE. Ey... I remember your / face.

RUTH. Oh god sorry.

LEE. For what?

RUTH. I really am sorry / for –

LEE. Nuthin to apologise for duck! She needed looking after. Saved me a job.

RUTH *smiles*.

RUTH. I'm Ruth.

LEE. Ruth!! I see, I see... Aww... What you on about Bex, she is pretty.

BEX. I didn't mean / like –

LEE. Anyhow, fuck the wankers! Tomorrow night. I'm having a party.

DILLON. Me and Bex were / gonna –

LEE. Gonna get the gear in. My treat.

DILLON. I was gonna take Bex out.

LEE. Save your fuckin P Dillon, party at ours man!

DILLON. But –

LEE. Gonna leave me on my tod are ya? On my birthday you little scrot?

DILLON. Nah, nah obviously if –

LEE. What you reckon Bex, got some flake that'll blow your lickle head off.

BEX. I dunno actually / if –

LEE. Thought we were friends Bex. Am I not your friend?

BEX. You are, yeah.

LEE. Tomorrow night at the caravan then. It's gonna be fuckin
lit! Let's say seven yeah? And I don't wanna be no third wheel
all night neither so bring a mate. You have got mates right?

RUTH. Um hello? That's me.

RUTH *laughs awkwardly.*

Joke. That was a. I was joking. We're not really friends at
the / moment.

LEE. Nah you're invited Ruth! I'm inviting you!

RUTH. Oh no I wasn't / saying –

BEX. Her dad wouldn't let her anyway.

RUTH. Well I don't have to tell him.

LEE. Ooooh naughty / Ruth!

BEX. But you don't dance or drink or / anything.

RUTH. You don't want me to come. / I get it.

LEE. Fuck what she wants! What do you want?

RUTH. It does sound like fun.

BEX. Oh my / god.

LEE. Ruth is fuckin / on it!

BEX. You won't like it.

RUTH. You said I was boring.

LEE. Bit harsh / Bex!

BEX. She wouldn't like it / there.

RUTH. This is me not being / boring.

LEE. Maybe Ruth is a secret mad-head!

RUTH. Maybe I am...

LEE. That's settled then!

BEX. Fucksake Ruth.

RUTH. What?

LEE. Come then Dillon. Go Aldi, get some beers in. In a bit ladies!

LEE *exits*. DILLON *is about to follow him…*

BEX. Dillon what the fuck?

DILLON. I'll still make it special. Promise. Message you later.

DILLON *kisses* BEX *on the cheek then follows his brother.* RUTH *anxiously smiles at* BEX.

RUTH. Am I coming? To the party? Is that what's happening?

BEX. Yeah.

RUTH. Ooh that's quite exciting.

BEX. Mm.

RUTH. Are you still angry with me?

BEX *rolls her eyes and shakes her head.*

My mum used to get really bad PMT, you know. Sometimes before her period she'd threaten to set the house alight with my dad asleep inside because his snoring made her so angry. Maybe you're just due on your period.

BEX. Maybe.

RUTH. Will you do my make-up for me?

BEX RESCUES RUTH

The following day, Saturday night.

The caravan. Music is coming from little speakers. DILLON is sat in a deckchair and BEX sits in his lap... RUTH is lying down on the grass, unseen.

DILLON. Got some little candles from Aldi. For the bedroom. For later.

BEX. Did ya?

DILLON. Swear down. So it's special n / that.

BEX. Where did Ruth go?

DILLON. Dunno, toilet?

BEX. Ruth...?

> RUTH *suddenly sits bolt up right wearing pineapple sunglasses.* LEE *appears from out the caravan and begins to go for a piss by the side of it.*

RUTH (*sort of singing*). Hello? Is it me you're looking / for?

BEX. Wheey! Here she is!

> RUTH *props the sunglasses on her head. Her pupils are huge.*

RUTH (*to* BEX). I'm back in the / game!!

LEE. Stevie's in Notts for one night / only!

DILLON. Why didn't you just piss in the actual toilet you dickhead?

LEE. I'll piss in your mouth if I fancy it Dillon.

RUTH. Urgh!

LEE. Sorry Stevie! That weren't for your / ears!

BEX. Stop being a knob Lee.

LEE. Oh shut up you little rat.

RUTH. Rats are actually really intelligent creatures.

LEE (*to* DILLON). Acting all cocky in front of your bird cos you wanna get a shag / innit…

DILLON. Shut up.

LEE. Wish me happy birthday / then.

RUTH. HAPPY / BIRTHDAY!

DILLON. Happy birthday.

LEE. I fucking love you Dillon!

> LEE *and* DILLON *have a friendly brotherly scrap then hug.*
>
> Oi help me get this fire started while I can still see straight.
>
> LEE *picks up a petrol can, the brothers disappear behind the caravan to start the fire.* RUTH *turns to* BEX, *suddenly very serious.*

RUTH. I know I don't really say it much or whatever. But you honestly mean so much to me.

BEX. You have said it quite a lot tonight.

RUTH. Cos you're basically like my fucking wand. You give me magic! Like whoooossshh! By the way. I didn't mean like you couldn't be a rat. Because I said they're *actually* intelligent. I wasn't meaning like you can't be a rat *because* they're intelligent. Because you can be a rat if you want to be. You ARE a rat! I just mean he was saying it like it was a bad thing but really. Rats are great!

BEX. Cool. Thanks Ruth.

RUTH. Anytime. Yeah. Anytime.

> DILLON *appears from behind the caravan.*

DILLON. Beer anyone?

RUTH. ME PLEASE!

> RUTH *is up bobbing to the music.* BEX *watches her.* DILLON *cracks open some beers.* LEE *appears, consumed by his mobile phone, texting.*
>
> Honestly changed my life so much because when I met you – oh my god, Holme Pierrepoint! White-water rafting!

Oh my god. Oh my god. And you were like – all like 'fuck vegans'. And I was like who the hell is this girl?! Cos you're so like. FUCK YOU. To the world. And that's really cool. Cos. You know. I'm so like: Wahh. And you're like: Rahh.

BEX. You need to drink some water.

RUTH. NO! Rum! Rahh! I'm being: Rahh.

BEX (*to* DILLON). She needs / some water!

RUTH. Someone dance with me! Please!

DILLON. Chill, she's / alright.

RUTH. Lee!! Dance with me! I'm being: Rahh!

LEE. What the fuck is Rahh?

RUTH. You know. Like: POW. Like: Oh hey I'm in the room, don't fuck with me. Like: Yeaaaaah biaaaatches you fuckin with me, I said ARE YOU FUCKIN WITH ME?! Like: you know, like loud or sort of like hey motherfuckers I've arrived. That kind of thing. You know: Rahh.

LEE. Riiiiigghhtt… Yeah. I get you now. / Rahh!

BEX. Ruth shut up you're so fucked!

RUTH. I know! I LOVE IT. I want another pill. Can I have another one please?

LEE. You're poppin em like Smarties / duck.

BEX. Don't give her another one! / She's fucked.

LEE. Oh gerrout of it. You can have another one if you want darling. Here.

LEE *gets a bag of pills out his pocket and gives one to* RUTH.

RUTH. I like you. You give me drugs. Drugs are naughty. I like drugs.

LEE's *mobile beeps, receiving a message, he reads it.*

Ooooh who's that?

DILLON. Best not be Dad.

LEE. I only text him.

RUTH. Text who?

DILLON. Lee bro! We made a / promise.

RUTH. Who did you text?

LEE. When I'm a dad Ruth. I'm / gonna be the –

RUTH. ARE YOU GONNA BE A DAD?!

LEE. If, I mean. I'd make sure I was the best fucking dad there ever was!

RUTH. Ooooooh yeah. You'd be like one of them cool dads.

LEE. Mine ain't even bothered to ring me!

RUTH. Oh no.

DILLON. Lee…

LEE. Is it too much to ask for a happy birthday from m'dad, is it Ruth?

RUTH. I think. No. That's what I / think.

DILLON. Lee just leave / it –

LEE. Shut up Dillon! I wanna hear what Stevie Wonder has to say / about it.

BEX. Ruth?

RUTH. About what?

BEX. Come sit / for a sec…

LEE. Is it too much to ask for your dad to wish you a happy fucking birthday?

RUTH. Yes. No. I mean. Wait, what was the question?

LEE. Do you love your dad Ruth?

RUTH. Yes.

BEX. Ruth.

LEE. I fucking hate my dad.

RUTH. Oh no that's / not –

LEE. I don't. I love him. I love him too much.

RUTH. It's very confusing isn't it? Feelings are very confusing.

DILLON. It's not that confusing. Basically Ruth, Dad can be a prick.

LEE. Shut your mouth Dillon! You don't fuckin understand! Cos it's not him right. It's me. I should have fuckin been somebody… Done something with my fuckin life. And look at me! Think I want to be hanging out with a bunch of teenagers on my birthday Dillon?! I'm fucking… It's not Dad's fault that I'm fucking… I'm fuckin nothing.

LEE breaks down. RUTH stops dancing and strokes LEE's back.

RUTH. You're not nothing Lee.

LEE. Sorry. I'm being a soppy cunt.

DILLON. No you're not.

LEE. I wasn't talking to you! I was talking to Ruth.

RUTH. It's good to be a soppy cunt sometimes. Let it out.

LEE. Dad doesn't have anyone else apart from us Ruth. I can't leave him. Even if he is a cunt.

RUTH. Well at least *you're* not a cunt Lee. I mean you're a soppy cunt but you're not a cunt cunt.

RUTH flicks her shades down and sways with her hands in the air, doing a Stevie Wonder impression.

Lee. Wait. Lee. Lee, who am I again? Who am I?

LEE chuckles.

LEE. Oh fucking hell… Stevie Wonder's / back!

RUTH (*sort of singing*). Rolling, rolling on the river!

LEE. That's Tina Turner you doughnut!

RUTH and LEE are both mashed and laughing together. RUTH sprawls herself across LEE as he starts to roll a joint. DILLON plugs some headphones into his mobile.

BEX. Dillon…

DILLON. Chill, she's havin a good time.

BEX. There's so much stuff in my head that I wanna say…

DILLON. Come here then, listen to this song. It's proper peng.

He offers BEX *his headphones.* BEX *looks at* RUTH *and* LEE, *then puts the earphones in. She nestles into* DILLON's *chest, he strokes her head.* LEE *lights his joint, he watches* RUTH *in amazement as he smokes, grinning and gurning his nut off.*

LEE. I bet you're in all the top sets at school aren't ya.

RUTH. Yeah.

LEE. And here you are mashed off your head on four pills in the middle of a field. You're fucking cool Ruth.

RUTH. I am yeah.

LEE. Bex said you were proper frigid. But you're a fucking laugh. You're a fucking nutter mate.

RUTH. Mmm.

RUTH *throws up on the tiny patch of grass between* LEE's *legs, narrowly missing his trainers.*

LEE. Ruth. Mate. You're lucky I like you. Cos I think you just chucked up on my Air Max.

RUTH. I'll lick them clean, I promise.

LEE. Come on then babe, let's get you cleaned up, have a shower if you want? Have a lickle lie-down?

RUTH *nods yes.* LEE *puts her arm around him, brings her to standing and guides her into the caravan.* BEX *suddenly takes a headphone out one ear and turns to* DILLON.

BEX. Do you love me Dillon?

DILLON. We haven't even had sex.

BEX. I don't think I can do this if you don't love me.

DILLON. –

68   LIT

BEX. Right.

DILLON. I do.

BEX. No I get it.

DILLON. I do, alright?

BEX. It's fine.

DILLON. Obviously I love you. Fuck.

Beat.

BEX. You never said it.

DILLON. Was gonna tell you later wasn't I. In bed with all the candles n that. Gone an ruined it now you bell-end.

BEX *looks at* DILLON, *then kisses him. They keep kissing, only pausing so he can undo his fly.* DILLON *looks around, sees no one is there.*

Suck me off.

BEX *goes to kiss him again. He pulls away.*

Please Bex.

BEX. Tell me you love me Dillon.

DILLON. I love you.

BEX *gets onto her knees.* DILLON *pushes her head aggressively towards his groin.* BEX *pulls away and looks around.*

BEX. Where's Ruth?

DILLON. Give me your hand.

Suddenly BEX *is on her feet, anxious.*

BEX. Where's Ruth Dillon?

DILLON. Toilet or / something.

BEX. Ruth?

BEX *goes to the caravan door, tries to open it, but it doesn't open. It's locked.*

Why is it locked Dillon?

DILLON. We were having a special moment? / Bex?

DILLON grabs her hand and holds her tight so she can't move and kisses her again. She pulls away.

BEX. Stop it Dillon. Why is the door / locked?

DILLON. I wanna finally have sex tonight Bex. I wanna to lose it to you.

He pulls her skirt up, tugs her knickers, she squirms and bangs at the caravan door.

BEX. Dillon stop it. Lee! Lee! / Lee! Open the door!

DILLON. Bex I told you I loved you and you can't let me just! I've waited so long / for this!

BEX is suddenly hysterical.

BEX. Get off me! Get off me Dillon! You're just like your fucking brother! She's in there with Lee! Ruth?! Ruth! Lee, let her out! Lee! Fucking open the door! Get out here now! Fucking please! Please Lee! Don't!

The caravan door slams open. LEE is stood there, looking confused.

Where is she!?

BEX runs into the caravan.

LEE. W'the fuck! Thought the fucking feds turned up! Just chucked all my gear in the septic tank you twat! Sort that piece out Dillon! What she / fucking playin at!

DILLON. Shut the fuck up Lee!

DILLON pushes LEE hard in the chest.

LEE. You what!

DILLON. Did you just try and fuck Ruth?!

LEE. Course I didn't!! She's a right state!

BEX exits the caravan with RUTH's arm round her neck; RUTH's just able to walk but she's out of it.

Ruth tell her / I didn't –

BEX. Get away from her!

LEE. Ruth!?

BEX. Don't fucking touch her!

> BEX *drags* RUTH *away from the caravan. The boys call after them.*

LEE. I didn't!

DILLON. Bex! Wait! He didn't –

MARK REJECTS BEX

Two days later, Tuesday late afternoon.

MARK *stands by his car, outside* BEX's *residential care home in town.*

MARK. Get in.

BEX. No.

MARK. Please just get in the car.

BEX. Were you just waiting for me? Cos that's / fucking –

MARK. I'm not doing this in the street.

BEX. I'll scream. I'll tell them / that you're –

MARK. Bex!

Beat.

You took her to the caravan didn't you?

BEX. We stayed here.

MARK. She came back stinking of smoke. A right state. / She –

BEX. We had a sleepover.

MARK. Do you think I'm an idiot Bex?

BEX. No.

MARK. Do you?

BEX. Obviously not.

MARK. What happened to my daughter?

BEX. I don't know.

MARK. She's hardly spoken a word the last couple days. She's locked herself in her room most of the day. She won't let me in. She doesn't want to go to school. She's got bruises all over her legs and. Just tell me what happened?!

BEX. I didn't want her to come. She wanted to come.

MARK. Bex!

BEX. He said he didn't.

MARK. Oh god.

BEX. He said he didn't touch her.

MARK. Fuck, fuck.

BEX. He promised he didn't.

MARK. Do you realise what you've done?!

BEX. –

MARK. Was this revenge?

BEX. Revenge for what?

MARK. Some messed-up twisted revenge cos you were upset that I wouldn't kiss you? Is that what / this was?

BEX. No!

MARK. I can't believe you seriously thought I wanted to / shag you!

BEX. It wasn't anything / to do with –

MARK. What planet are you on?!

Beat.

BEX. Yeah but.

MARK. What?

BEX. You told me I was beautiful.

MARK. Jesus Bex I didn't / mean –

BEX. You looked at me like...

MARK. I'm not like them Bex!

BEX. No but...

MARK. I'm not them!

BEX. You thought about it. You did. I know you did.

Silence.

MARK. Stay away from our home.

BEX. Can you tell her I'm sorry?

MARK. You hear me?!

BEX. Please tell her.

MARK. Stay away from Ruth.

BEX. I'm so sorry.

MARK. No wonder nobody wants you.

MARK *slams his car door shut and drives off.* BEX *is alone.*

BEX BURNS THE PAST

Later that night.

The caravan, the lights are on. BEX *is pouring petrol over the walls of the caravan, hysterical.*

BEX. Get out! Fucking get out! Get the fuck out!

> *Suddenly the doors bang open and* LEE *steps out, followed by* DILLON. *As they open the door* BEX *dashes petrol over* LEE, *catching* DILLON *too. She takes a lighter out her pocket.*

LEE. What the fuck?! Whoa!! Bex! What the fuck are / you doing!?

BEX. Don't come / near me!

DILLON. Bex! What's happened?

LEE. Whoa whoa whoa!

BEX. I swear to / fucking God!

DILLON. Bex calm down!

BEX. I'll light you!

DILLON. Look / at me.

BEX. I'll fucking / light you!

LEE. Alright! / Alright!

BEX. What did you do to her?

DILLON. He swore / to me!

LEE. To who?!

BEX. To Ruth! What did / you do to Ruth!

LEE. I didn't fucking / touch her!

BEX. You did!

DILLON. I've been tryin to / call you!

LEE. What the fuck has she been sayin?!

BEX. Nothing! She can't –

DILLON. He didn't / Bex!

BEX. She can't / remember.

LEE. I swear I didn't Bex! I'm not that kind of man!

BEX. You're not that kind of man?!

LEE. No! I wouldn't fucking do that! I wouldn't shag a bird who can't / speak! Fucksake!

BEX. You're not that / kind of man?!

DILLON. Bex please.

LEE. Is that what you think of me / Bex?!

BEX. But you did that to / me, Lee?!

LEE. I promise you Bex I didn't / touch Ruth!

BEX. You did to her exactly like what you did to me.

    Beat.

LEE. What I did to you?

BEX. Do you think I wanted to / do that?

DILLON. Bex, it's all in the / past.

LEE. Do what?

BEX. You know / what?!

DILLON. Please Bex we can't change / it now!

BEX. I think about it every fucking / day!

DILLON. You were both / off your head.

LEE. What the fuck do you mean what I DID to you?

BEX. Don't you dare / fucking! Oh my god.

DILLON. Bex! Calm the fuck / down!

LEE. What I DID to / you?

BEX. Oh my god.

LEE. You fucking wanted it you dirty little slag!

DILLON. Lee don't!

BEX. Oh my god.

LEE. You were begging for my cock. Fucking pleading for it
you filthy / little cunt.

BEX. Shut the fuck up!

LEE. Are you calling me a fucking rapist?! Is that seriously
what you're / saying?!

BEX. Shut the fuck up! Shut the fuck up! I swear to god I will
fucking spark this and burn you! I will light you, you
fucking cunt!

BEX *holds the lighter out ready to spark it. The boys fall
silent. Heavy breathing.*

What you did to me. What you did to me was. You're a rapist.
That's / what –

LEE. You didn't say no!

BEX. I swear to fucking god!

LEE *shuts up.*

How can you even! Try and think that wasn't fucking. I think
about it every single day. And it makes me feel…

DILLON. Bex.

BEX. It makes me feel…

DILLON. I'm so / sorry.

BEX. Fucking admit / it Lee!

LEE. You wanted / it!

DILLON. Shut the fuck up Lee!

BEX. I wanted it?! I wanted it?! Can you / hear yourself?!

DILLON. Bex please.

BEX. It was meant to be me and you Dillon.

DILLON. I know.

BEX. It was meant to be me and you.

DILLON. I should have stopped it.

BEX. I thought I loved you / Dillon.

DILLON. I'm so sorry / Bex.

LEE. You're a filthy little slag.

DILLON. I love you.

BEX *sparks the lighter. The flame burns in front of the boys.*

Whoa. Bex, Bex, / Bex.

LEE. Bex don't be a silly bitch.

BEX. You don't love me Dillon. You just don't.

The lighter sparks. Excruciating screams are engulfed in flames.

They echo in BEX*'s head as time passes.*

Then silence.

SYLVIA VISITS BEX

Seven months later. Late April.

A visiting room in Rainsbrook Secure Training Centre in Rugby.
SYLVIA *sits at a table looking nervous. After a short while,*
BEX *appears. She's showing a large pregnancy bump.* SYLVIA
stands, looks at the bump and then at BEX. *They are being
observed by a Rainsbrook officer.*

SYLVIA. You're [pregnant]…?

BEX. Y'don't have to stand. I'm not the Queen.

SYLVIA. God Bex.

BEX. Thought you weren't gonna come.

SYLVIA. You're huge.

BEX. Bit rude.

SYLVIA. Sorry. I just mean you should have told me. I would
have bought something to say congratulations or… Sorry.

They both sit in silence for a moment.

I was surprised that you got in touch. That you were able to
get in touch.

BEX. They posted it for me.

SYLVIA. Right, I see.

BEX. They don't normally allow / contact [with ex-foster
parents].

SYLVIA. No.

BEX. But I needed / to um… [talk to you about something.]

SYLVIA. No I didn't think so.

An awkward beat.

BEX. Not like I can start stalking you though is it?

SYLVIA. –

BEX. Bit tricky to stalk someone when you're in prison.

An awkward beat.

Got here alright then?

SYLVIA. Yes it was a fairly easy route actually. Straight down the A46, then onto the M1.

BEX. Was expecting y'to moan. Know how much you hate driving.

An awkward beat.

Cats still alive?

SYLVIA. Mm.

BEX. Thought Bilbo might be dead by now.

An awkward beat.

How's the dating scene going?

SYLVIA. Oh you know…

BEX. Met any men with hair yet?

SYLVIA. I have actually.

BEX. Shit the bed. Who is he?

SYLVIA. It's just early stages.

BEX. What's his name then?

SYLVIA. I'm not really sure if um…

BEX. What?

SYLVIA. So what have you been up to? I mean. I know you're here obviously but, I mean, you know, I dunno, do you have things to do or, oh god I don't know why I asked that question, that was a really stupid thing to ask…

BEX. Tryna get me to finish my GCSEs. Making pancakes in food tech later.

SYLVIA. Oh well that's good isn't it.

BEX. Not really. I hate pancakes.

An awkward beat.

You look better.

SYLVIA. I am.

BEX. They got you on pills or summit?

SYLVIA. No. All natural.

BEX. That's good then.

SYLVIA. Had some therapy and um. I've started a reiki course.
Apparently I've got the gift.

BEX. Fuck's that?

SYLVIA. Healing. I'm training to become a healer.

BEX. Right… Sure you're not still a nutjob? Cos that sounds
a / bit…

SYLVIA. Officially not a nutjob. Got a letter from the doctor to
prove it. Been back at work three months now.

An awkward beat.

Are you okay?

BEX. Apart from being bored out my arse, yeah, suppose.

SYLVIA. Oh. Well. I didn't know if you would want it but um.
I actually got in touch with Ruth / and –

BEX. What?

SYLVIA. I know you might feel a bit. I don't know. About / it
but –

BEX. Why the fuck would you do that?

SYLVIA. I suppose, I didn't understand… Why you / would…

BEX. What did she say to you about me?

SYLVIA. Well I told her that you'd sent me a letter / and that I
was –

BEX. Fucking hell / Sylvia.

SYLVIA. No hang on now. Hear me out. I know, that was your
friendship and maybe it wasn't my place but. I told her I was
coming to see you / and –

BEX. Oh my god you're a / dick.

SYLVIA. She gave me something to give to you.

BEX. –

SYLVIA. It's in the drop box. It's a book. For you to read. She
    said she thought you might be bored so.

BEX. –

SYLVIA. She said you should have enough time to finish it.
    I think it was sort of a joke but I didn't really laugh. I
    couldn't really find it. Funny. I don't think she meant it in
    a bad way but.

    There's no drugs in it or anything. They checked all the pages.

BEX. Thanks. Tell her.

    SYLVIA *smiles for the first time*.

SYLVIA. How far gone are you?

BEX. Eight months.

SYLVIA. Do you know if it's a boy or a girl?

BEX. Girl.

SYLVIA. Oh that's good, isn't it? I mean if it was a boy that
    would be too but…

    Beat.

    Is it… is it Dillon's baby?

BEX. Thought Tracey woulda let you read my case report.

SYLVIA. I only know what was in the local paper.

BEX. Yeah well.

SYLVIA. They didn't use your name or anything / but –

BEX. It probably weren't the whole story. Was it.

    An uncomfortable silence.

SYLVIA. So how much longer do you um…

BEX. My lawyer's demanding a community order, but.

SYLVIA. That sounds good?

BEX. Not exactly gonna count my chickens.

SYLVIA. Mm.

BEX. But cos of my age, and cos of Dillon's statement, he reckons I could get the sentence reduced to four years.

SYLVIA. I see.

BEX. W'good behaviour I could be out in two.

Beat.

SYLVIA. What happens to her when she's born?

BEX. Got a mother-and-baby unit here, for girls w'babies n that. I'm being assessed so.

SYLVIA. Oh right?

BEX. Depends if there's space for me, should find out next week. It'll just be on a temporary placement. If there is one. While I wait for my sentence. Everything takes so long.

SYLVIA. Mm.

BEX. But if I do get a place on MBU then I can keep her inside with me after the birth. Bond with her n that. Allowed eighteen months max.

SYLVIA. And after the eighteen months…?

BEX. They take her. Then they take her away from me basically.

An uncomfortable beat.

I have to go to this big board meeting thing next week with bare important people.

SYLVIA. Board meeting?

BEX. Yeah, where they decide what happens to her basically. Said it might be tricky, cos I'm only fifteen. I'm a 'vulnerable child' apparently. They've all been talking about me, which you'd think I'd love but. Reckon it's gonna be like *X Factor* or summit, stood there presenting them with all my hopes and dreams of being a mum an that. And then. Then they'll just like shit all over them probably.

Beat.

Must have endless paperwork on me.

SYLVIA. Mm.

BEX. I keep telling them, you know about the environmental crisis, save the trees, I'm really not that important but.

Apparently she's already got a social worker. She ain't even born yet and she's got a fuckin social worker. It's mad innit?

SYLVIA. –

BEX. They take everything into consideration basically and then make a decision that's in the best interest of the child.

SYLVIA. Of course, yeah.

An awkward beat.

So you... You would want to be a mum... when you get out?

BEX. Yeah. It's a girl so... Yeah. Obviously.

But I can't really think about it can I? Probs not gonna happen.

SYLVIA. And that's. That's it is it?

Beat.

BEX. Well I... I guess / if...

SYLVIA. Because that's...

BEX. If I had a family or a guardian or whatever, who wanted to look after her. While I / was –

SYLVIA. Oh no. / Bex.

BEX. Inside. Until I got / out.

SYLVIA. Did you want me to...

BEX. Most girls have two named guardians when they go in MBU.

SYLVIA. You really should have explained that in the letter.

BEX. They're tryna push for her to be removed at birth Sylvia.

SYLVIA. Oh / god.

BEX. They'll take her away from me literally within six hours after giving birth to her.

SYLVIA. Bex.

BEX. In the fucking hospital but.

SYLVIA. Is that why you wrote / to me?

BEX. I'm fighting it basically.

SYLVIA. To ask me to look after your baby?

BEX. Cos the thing is, if I don't have anyone to look after her while I'm serving the rest of my sentence then she'll have to go into foster care / so.

SYLVIA. Because that's a… it's a big thing. A big ask. / I mean I just don't…

BEX. Nah it's fine. I get it, it's fine. Honestly it's… I'm not expecting you to just. Fucking. Whatever. I haven't seen you for. You know. I haven't seen you since. You've obviously got a new life with your cats and your boyfriend and your magic healing shit so.

An uncomfortable silence.

SYLVIA. I'll write to you again if you'd like?

BEX. Yeah alright.

SYLVIA. It'll be like we're pen pals.

BEX. Not really.

SYLVIA. No. Sorry.

SYLVIA *gets up to leave.*

BEX. People say that a lot.

SYLVIA. I really am.

BEX. Sorry.

Late May. One month later. We are back at the birthing ward in hospital. SYLVIA's gone. BEX speaks to Amy, who's lying in a plastic neonatal cot.

Most the time they ain't saying it for you. Like they're just desperate to say summit to fill the silence and it's the only thing what's left. But it don't mean nothing, does it. Don't change nothing.

BEX *stares at her Amy.*

Look at ya just sleeping there like that, like you ain't got a
care in the world. You're so fucking beautiful. Makes this
harder, you know. Can't quite believe you came outta me.
Like only a few hours ago you were inside me. How the hell
has something that beautiful come outta me. That's mad that
is. I'm a mum. I'm actually a mum. Like what the fuck: I'm
a mum.

Think I've been waiting to love you my whole life. Like it's
just been building up and up, tryna find where the fuck all
this love should go.

God I wanna hold ya. So bad. Wanna feel your soft peachy
skin on mine. But I can't. Cos I'm scared. Scared to cuddle
ya. In case I can't let go.

Dunno why but. Keep thinkin about my mum. Your nannar,
yeah. God, she would have proper loved you.

Wonder if she'd say sorry if she could.

Jesus I'm chatting so much shit. Must be them meds they
gave me. Tripping me out.

Beat.

They keep telling me this is the best thing for ya. But it's not
like I got a choice is it? So if you wanna grow up and hate
me, like that's fine, join the queue.

Suppose I hope one day you can forgive me though, cos.

I am like. Sorry.

Sounds like just another fucking empty word when I say it
out loud but. I just – see I'm worried, I just hope you don't
think that I want you to leave, think I'm abandoning ya, cos
I'm not. I did fight. I wanted to keep you inside with me,
least till eighteen months, wanted to start raising ya myself.
God I tried so fucking hard to get them to let me keep ya but.
Nothing I ever said was good enough. Saying all this shit
like I'm a child myself, I'm too much of a risk. Such
absolute fucking bullshit. It might not have been perfect but
it woulda been something. And I get it. Like. I do get that

you deserve to be in the world. Obviously. Seeing things for
the first time like. Post boxes... dogs... pet shops n stuff.
And the seaside. Maybe you can start going swimming, see
I couldn't teach ya that could I? But maybe someone will.
And they'll get you them tiny little armbands –

I'm not gonna be there the first time you wear tiny fucking
armbands.

Beat.

They best fucking look after ya properly. You're so tiny.
Gonna drive me mad not knowing where you are, what
you're doing. Cos there's some sick fucking people in this
world Amy and I'm. I'm not gonna be there to protect ya.
But my god, if anything happens to you. I'll fucking. I'd kill
em, I would, I'd fuckin kill em, I'd. But that's it innit. I'm
gonna go back on that wing, everyone talking, saying I
fucked up. Shit mother. But. I'm gonna think about you
every single day. Imagine you lying there. Imagining your
little face. You just got no idea.

Can't explain how much I... [love you.]

It hurts.

I just love you so fucking much.

Silence.

How can I love you this much when you only been in my life
for five fucking hours?

But it's not long though. It's not long. Gonna keep my head
down. Be out in a couple years. You'll only be like, what
two? Maybe when you grow up you won't even remember
all this. And we'll be back together. Proper. In our own little
cottage or summit. Gloucestershire or whatever, anywhere,
we could go anywhere. And it's like, that's when my life will
start. Real life, proper life, this life I can imagine, like
fucking... Maybe by then I'll have learnt summit. Like how
to cook and stuff so I can teach ya. Like proper mummy
cooking. Vegetables n shit. Random stuff in jars, with little
labels saying the date I made it stuck to the side. Like what
Sylvia used to do.

I'm gonna be the best fucking mum there ever was.

Cos everything's gonna be…

Everything is gonna be just.

It's gonna be fucking…

Beat.

I'm gonna prove them wrong, Amy. Just you watch.

BEX *looks directly at the audience, addressing them for the first time.*

Cos I bet you all think I'll not amount to much. Don't ya?

But, fuck it.

I might even learn how to make jam.

A Nick Hern Book

LIT first published in Great Britain as a paperback original in 2019 by Nick Hern Books Limited, The Glasshouse, 49a Goldhawk Road, London W12 8QP, in association with HighTide Theatre and Nottingham Playhouse

LIT copyright © 2019 Sophie Ellerby

Cover image by Craig Sugden

Designed and typeset by Nick Hern Books, London
Printed in the UK by Mimeo Ltd, Huntingdon, Cambridgeshire PE29 6XX

A CIP catalogue record for this book is available from the British Library

ISBN 978 1 84842 892 8